The Marche

Julius Honnor

D1340315

9/2245159

Credits

Footprint credits
Editor: Nicola Gibbs
Production and layout: Emma Bryers
Maps: Kevin Feeney
Cover: Pepi Bluck

Publisher: Patrick Dawson
Managing Editor: Felicity Laughton
Advertising: Elizabeth Taylor
Sales and marketing: Kirsty Holmes

Photography credits
Front cover: Clodio/Dreamstime.com
Back cover: Alexander Tolstykh/
Shutterstock.com

Printed in Great Britain by CPI Antony Rowe,
Chippenham, Wiltshire

MIX
Paper from
responsible sources
FSC
www.fsc.org FSC® C013604

Every effort has been made to ensure that
the facts in this guidebook are accurate.
However, travellers should still obtain advice
from consulates, airlines, etc, about travel
and visa requirements before travelling.
The authors and publishers cannot accept
responsibility for any loss, injury or
inconvenience however caused.

Publishing information
Footprint *Focus The Marche*
1st edition
© Footprint Handbooks Ltd
April 2013

ISBN: 978 1 909268 10 4
CIP DATA: A catalogue record for this book
is available from the British Library

® Footprint Handbooks and the Footprint
mark are a registered trademark of
Footprint Handbooks Ltd

Published by Footprint
6 Riverside Court
Lower Bristol Road
Bath BA2 3DZ, UK
T +44 (0)1225 469141
F +44 (0)1225 469461
footprinttravelguides.com

Distributed in the USA by Globe Pequot
Press, Guilford, Connecticut

All rights reserved. No part of this
publication may be reproduced, stored
in a retrieval system, or transmitted, in
any form or by any means, electronic,
mechanical, photocopying, recording,
or otherwise without the prior permission
of Footprint Handbooks Ltd.

The content of Footprint *Focus The Marche*
has been taken directly from Footprint's
Umbria & Marche guide, which was
researched and written by Julius Honnor.

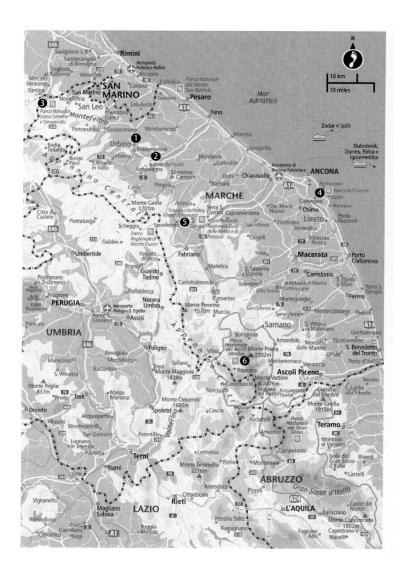

Marche, the ancient land of the Picenes, has hills aplenty – sometimes topped with medieval towns and castles – as well as mountains and a Mediterranean coast.

From ancient Rome to Raphael, there's a wealth of historical and artistic treasures. Urbino, in northern Marche, is one of the Italian Renaissance's most celebrated towns, with steep hills, grand architecture and views to compete with any in Italy. To the south, Macerata has a famous opera festival and a strange ancient sport all of its own, while Ascoli Piceno has breathtakingly beautiful piazzas and a lively contemporary art scene.

Ascoli Piceno, Macerata and Urbino all have universities, which add some youthful spice to the cultural mix. On the coast, Ancona, Pesaro and Fano have their own distinct style as a result of trade, shipping and fishing.

The landscape is stunning, with enormous panoramic vistas around every corner. The spine of the region, the Apennine range – snow-capped in winter then enrobed in spring flowers – makes ideal walking country.

Alternatively, laze on a sandy Adriatic beach with great local wine and delicious pasta, flavoured with the mysterious truffles that grow under the roots of the region's trees.

Wherever you go in Marche, non-Italians are a rarity, making it a wonderful opportunity to get to know Italy with all its attractions and almost none of the tourist trappings.

Planning your trip

Best time to visit Marche

Winter in Marche is cold with temperatures dropping close to freezing at night. Snowfall is common across the region, especially at higher altitudes, where cross-country skiing is popular. However, January is the second driest month and the weather is often crisp and sunny. **Carnevale**, in February, is an especially big deal in Ascoli Piceno (see page 14) where there's a week of feasting and processions.

Spring can be slow in arriving, especially at higher altitudes where the snow lingers. Even at lower levels the temperature rarely hits 15°C. Easter is celebrated with plenty of pomp and ceremony. At night the temperature drops and there can still be frosts, but the days are becoming warmer.

As the snows melt, the mountains become covered in a carpet of wild flowers. Timing depends on the weather, but crocuses, blue squill, orchids and narcissi usually flower first, followed by geraniums, buttercups, peonies and tulips in June and then cornflowers, daisies and poppies. Butterflies also enjoy the show. At lower levels May is usually pleasantly warm with maximum temperatures averaging 22°C.

By June, the last remnants of snow in the high mountains melt away as the average maximum temperature climbs to 26°C and the region's many summer festivals get under way. In July the average maximum temperature is 29°C but can reach the mid-30s. However, nights are seldom oppressively warm and the hills offer a cool respite. The beaches become busy with italians and northern Europeans on their summer holidays and ice creams become an almost obligatory part of the evening *passeggiata*. Many towns host age-old celebrations, often with a medieval theme.

In August the inland towns empty as people head to the coast; you may have to fight to get a beach umbrella. Hot, sunny weather predominates, punctuated by occasional heavy thunderstorms. Many of the locals who stay behind are involved in traditional festivals, and improvised outdoor eateries spring up in the medieval hill towns as figs ripen and shops fill with delicious local tomatoes. On 15 August Italy comes to a complete standstill for **Ferragosto** (see page 14).

By autumn, the heat of summer tails off and there are mists in the mornings over the valleys, as Italians troop back to work. Nights are often cold and the first snows may fall on the peaks of the Sibillini. Grapes are havested and porcini mushrooms, gathered from the woods, become increasingly popular on restaurant menus.

November is usually the wettest month; the average temperature drops below 10°C for the first time but there can still be some pleasantly warm days. The first new olive oil pressings become available from the year's crop and are best consumed fresh.

Snow is possible in December though white Christmases are only likely at higher levels. On average the temperature falls to only 9°C but December is usually drier than November and somtimes seasonally crisp, frosty weather creates a festive mood. **Capodanno** (New Year) is welcomed with fireworks, feasting and lentil soup.

Don't miss...

Getting to Marche

Air

From UK and Ireland Flights to Milan or Rome depart from UK and Irish destinations frequently. Alternatively, fly right to the heart of Marche with **Ryanair** ① *www.ryanair. com*, which flies from London Stansted to Ancona four times a week in winter and daily in summer. There are also Ryanair flights to Perugia, across the Apennines in Umbria, three times a week in winter, five times a week in summer. Other central Italian regional airports such as Bologna, Pisa and Rimini are also possible arrival points.

From North America There are no direct flights to Marche from North America; the closest connections are via Rome or Milan. **Continental**, **American Airlines** and **Delta** fly direct from New York to Rome Fiumicino and Milan. **Delta** also flies to both cities from Toronto via New York.

From rest of Europe Airports in Rome and Milan are well connected to every major European city.

Airport information Ancona Falconara ① *T071-28271, www.aeroportomarche.com*. A small provincial airport, Ancona Falconara is connected to the train station in the town centre by hourly bus J (**Conerobus** ① *T071-283 7411, www.conerobus.it*), which takes around 35 minutes and costs €1.70 – buy tickets from the news stand in the Departures hall. There is also a train station at the airport, but services are infrequent. **Taxis** ① *T071-918221*, to the centre of Ancona cost around €35 and take 30 minutes. Car rental offices include **Avis, Hertz, Europcar, Maggiore** and **Sixt**.

Rail

Rail journeys involve taking the **Eurostar** to Paris, then onwards overnight sleepers to the most convenient Italian rail hubs: Milan (four hours from Ancona), Rome (three hours) or Bologna (two hours). For international tickets and information contact **Rail Europe** ① *T0870-584 8848, www.raileurope.com*. For Italian train information search **Trenitalia** ① *T06-6847 5475, www.trenitalia.it*. **Motorail** ① *www.autoslaaptrein.nl*, services run from the Netherlands to Livorno or Bologna, allowing you to drive on and drive off.

Road

Bus/coach Eurolines ① *T08717-818178, www.eurolines.co.uk*, operates three services per week from London Victoria to Milan, taking around 28 hours. Prices start at £71 return.

Car The 1700-km journey from London to Ancona will take about 16 hours' driving time. The A1 *autostrade* (motorway) that splices Italy vertically and then the A14 along the Adriatic coast provide a fairly direct route to Ancona (a four-hour drive from Milan).

Transport in Marche

The major towns along the coast are well connected by train and there's also a branch line to Ascoli Piceno and a trans-Apennine route to Foligno in Umbria and beyond. Train stations are often at the peripheries of towns, however, meaning that a bus journey or taxi ride is necessary to reach the town centre. Buses also run to most places, though they are often infrequent, and just about non-existent on Sundays. For the freedom to go to more out-of-the-way places, when you want, a car is invaluable, especially if you plan to stay in an *agriturismo* in the countryside.

Touring Club Italiano produce good general maps of the area. For more detail, **Kompass** do a series of walking and cycling maps that cover some of the region's most popular areas. For real detail of local areas, maps produced by the **Club Alpino Italiano** are hard to beat, but equally hard to get hold of, though they can usually be found in towns on the edges of national and regional parks.

Rail

Three main lines serve central Italy: the Rome to Ancona line, via Spoleto and Foligno; the Rome to Florence line up the Tiber Valley, via Orvieto; and the Adriatic coastline. Fast Eurostar trains run along all of these routes, as well as ordinary (and cheaper) regional trains.

Tickets are cheap, though the price is approximately double for the faster, more comfortable **Eurostar** trains. Tickets can be booked at www.trenitalia.com and the website has timetables and prices in English. Some examples of journey times and single, second-class fares are: Ancona to Spoleto, two hours 15 minutes, €9.25; Ancona to Ascoli Piceno, one hour 40 minutes, €6.95.

Amica fares are cheaper advance tickets (if you can find one), flexi fare costs more but is flexible, and standard fare is just that. Rail passes are available but are not always cheaper as a surcharge is added. In general, it's cheaper and more convenient to book online or at ticket machines for the journeys you need to take. When using a service such as Eurostar Italia or InterCity, advance booking is advised.

On many Italian trains it's possible to travel 'ticketless', meaning you get on the train and quote your booking reference when the conductor comes round. Otherwise, you must validate train tickets at the yellow stamping machines before boarding.

Road

Bicycle A mountain bike is a good way of seeing some of the region's countryside, but mostly the towns are too hilly and cobbled for bikes to be much use for getting around. Towns are also generally small enough for you to be able to walk anywhere fairly quickly. Outside of the towns, Italians are keen weekend lycra wearers, but it hasn't done anything to make cycling on the roads any safer.

Bus To reach Urbino, **Adriabus** ① *www.amibus.it*, operates a service every hour or so from Pesaro station, taking about 50 minutes, and another slower one that takes around 65 minutes. Buses mainly run from outside, or at least near, train stations.

Car EU nationals taking their own car need to have an International Insurance Certificate (also known as a *Carte Verde*). Those holding a non-EU licence also need to take an International Driving Permit with them. Unleaded petrol is *benzina*, diesel is *gasolio*.

Italy has strict laws on drink driving: steer clear of alcohol to be safe. The use of mobile telephones while driving is illegal. Other nuances of Italian road law include children under 1.5 m required to be in the back of the car and that a reflective jacket must be worn if your car breaks down on the carriageway in poor visibility. Make sure you've got one. On-the-spot fines for minor traffic offences are not uncommon – typically they will set you back €150-250. Always get a receipt if you incur one.

Speed limits are 130 kph (motorway), 110 kph (dual carriageway) and 50 kph (town). Limits are 20 kph lower on motorways and dual carriageways when the road is wet. *Autostrade* (motorways) are toll roads, so keep cash in the car as a backup even though you can use credit cards on the blue 'viacard' gates. **Autostrade** ① *T055-420 3200, www.autostrade.it*, provides information on motorways in Italy, and **Automobile Club d'Italia (ACI)** ① *T06-49981, www.aci.it*, provides general driving information. ACI offers roadside assistance with English-speaking operators on T116.

Be aware that there are restrictions on driving in historic city centres, indicated by signs with black letters ZTL (*zona a traffico limitato*) on a yellow background. If you pass these signs, your registration number may be caught and a fine will wing its way to you. If your hotel is in the centre of town, you may be entitled to an official pass – contact your hotel or car hire company. However, this pass is not universal and allows access to the hotel only.

Car hire Car hire is available at all of Italy's international airports and many domestic airports. You will probably wish to book the car before you arrive in the country, and it's best to do so for popular destinations and at busy times of year. Check in advance the opening times of the car hire office.

Car hire comparison websites and agents are a good place to start a search for the best deals. Try www.holidayautos.co.uk or www.carrentals.co.uk.

Check what each hire company requires from you. Some companies will ask for an International Driving Licence, alongside your normal driving licence, if the language of your licence is different to that of the country you're renting the car in. Others are content with an EU licence. You'll need to produce a credit card for most companies. If you book ahead, make sure that the named credit card holder is the same as the person renting and driving the car to avoid any problems. Most companies have a lower age limit of 21 years and require that you've held your licence for at least a year. Many have a young driver surcharge for those under 25. Confirm insurance and any damage waiver charges and keep all your documents with you when you drive.

Price codes

Where to stay

€€€€ over €300   €€€ €200-300

€€ €100-200   € under €100

Price codes refer to the cost of a double room for a one-night stay in high season.

Restaurants

€€€ over €30   €€ €20-30   € under €20

Price codes refer to the cost of a two-course meal with a drink for one person, including service and cover charge.

Where to stay in Marche

With an *agriturismo* or villa for rent on nearly every hillside, old town hotels sprucing themselves up and ancient castles and abbeys reinventing themselves as places to stay, there are plenty of good accommodation options in Marche. *Agriturismi* and villas are difficult to access without your own transport, though some will arrange to pick you up from a station. Staying in one of the major centres gives access to a good transport network. Wherever you are, a car gives you the invaluable freedom to explore, and none of the distances are enormous, though journeys can be slow. Rural accommodation just outside one of the smaller towns with your own transport might be the best of all worlds. Visit www.bellaumbria.net for some good accommodation listings.

Agriturismi

No longer a new phenomenon in Italy, the stay-on-a-farm concept is beginning to mature. Though there are still plenty of places where the accommodation is fairly plain – not much more than a room with a bed – others are moving upmarket and branching out to specialize in cookery courses, wine tasting, horse riding and even dog training. Vineyards are also beginning to get in on the act, with some offering accommodation as well as guided tours.

In order to qualify as an *agriturismo*, places have to produce a certain amount of their own food. Many are organic, and often this means that meals will include homegrown fruit and vegetables and hand-reared meat. Olive oil, wine and honey are almost always local and abundant. Rural accommodation that doesn't also produce its own food used to be called a country house, but has now been reclassified as *turismo rurale*. Prices for *agriturismi* are usually given per person, and start at around €30 per night – more like €45 for the smarter places. Half board is often a good deal: expect to add around €20 per person for a meal that would probably cost at least €30 in a restaurant.

Many *agriturismi* close in the winter, and may impose a minimum stay in the summer. Increasing numbers have websites, but the small nature of these businesses means that they can be hard to find. A few of the best are in this guide, but there are hundreds of others: www.agriturismo.it/en or www.agriturismo.net/marches are good places to start a search. Local tourist information websites will usually have lists and links too.

Si sposa

Going to Italy to get married in Tuscany is now an old story, and a whole industry has grown up around it. In Marche it's much more unusual, meaning that you may have to work a little harder to find a venue, but also that you may end up feeling more special.

It's not a cheap option, but you'll have a stunningly memorable venue and a backdrop to match. A handful of places are set up for foreign weddings, such as **Pietrarubbia** (see page 25) on the edge of the Sasso Simone e Simoncello regional park in Marche. Some venues have their own chapels, often centuries-old buildings that once served long-abandoned hillltop villages, and the best will organize everything for you – from the service to evening yoga and massage sessions. For some organizational assistance, try **Love and Lord** (www.loveandlord.com) in the UK.

Hotels

The region's hotels are often not especially stylish; whereas *agriturismi* have revitalized rural tourism, many town hotels have changed little in the last 30 years and are looking rather stale. Some are wonderful grand old relics, however, and others are bucking the trend and becoming chic and modern, using their old spaces in new and creative ways.

Some of the most interesting places to stay are converted buildings such as old abbeys: **San Domenico** in Urbino (see page 34) offers breakfast in the cloisters.

Hotels can be relatively expensive for what you get – expect to pay around €100 a night for a double room with a reasonable level of comfort.

Self-catering

Renting a villa gives you the option of more independence and privacy. Many also have swimming pools. For a family or a small number of people the option of a villa can work out cheaper than staying in a hotel; if you are a group of 10 or so, the savings are greater, and there are some spectacular places to stay.

Good websites to search on include www.holidaylettings.co.uk, which has plenty of choice in Marche, and **Le Marche Explorer**, www.le-marche-explorer.com.

Food and drink in Marche

Marche is known for its uncomplicated but delicious cuisine. Pasta and gnocchi, usually home-made, are delicious, often served with a simple tomato and wild boar sauce, or with local pecorino cheese. Marche's coast means it tends to specialize in seafood, especially in seaside towns. Freshwater fish and eels from the lakes and rivers are sometimes found on menus too. Lentils are grown locally, especially in the Sibillini Mountains, and grains often feature in soups. Most ingredients are local, often supplied by small, sometimes organic producers. Tasty radicchio, the sweetest tomatoes and peppery rocket will make a fantastic salad, and if you're making a picnic there are plenty of great ingredients to buy.

Apreitivi Increasingly common is the *aperitivo milanese*: an early evening beer, glass of prosecco, or Campari and soda comes with a help-yourself buffet of meats, cheeses, and even plates of pasta. Most places will offer bowls of crisps and peanuts at least.

Biscuits and desserts Marche is not great for desserts, with a few exceptions. Most towns have a good ice-cream maker or two, but in many restaurants desserts will not be home-made. There are, however, some excellent biscuits to look out for. Most commonly, *tozzetti*, a hard, heavy almond biscuit, similar to the Tuscan *cantucci*, are sold along with *vin santo*, into which they should be dipped. A *digestivo* – a glass of something alcoholic to aid digestion – is commonly drunk at the end of a meal. Sweet dessert wines can be very good, and home-made grappa can sometimes be found, along with *amari* – bitter concoctions that supposedly once had medicinal uses. In and around Macerata and Ascoli Piceno in particular, age-old recipes are passed down and sworn by. *Nocino*, walnut liqueur, is another to look out for.

Bread Traditionally made without salt, bread in the region tends to come in large loaves, which are sometimes still baked in a traditional wood oven (ask for *pane al forno*). Because it goes stale quickly, it is often bought in half, or even quarter loaves. Yesterday's leftovers are often used to make *panzanella*, a tomato and bread salad. Saltless bread can take some getting used to, but it can also be delicious, allowing the natural sweetness of the grain to emerge. The story goes that saltless bread developed as a reaction to the Salt War against the papacy in the 16th century.

Cheese Cheese in Marche is mainly pecorino, of which there is a large variety. Made from sheep's milk, or a blend of milk from sheep and goats, its strength varies depending on how long it has been aged. You may find it matured in red wine, to give flavour and a coloured rind. Moist when young, the matured cheese (*stagionato*) becomes increasingly crumbly.

The story goes that the first *formaggio di fossa* ('trench cheese') was created largely by chance, when pecorino was removed from harm's way in wartime and buried underground in the Talamello area of Marche. Not only does the cheese undergo a special kind of fermentation in these conditions, but in the few places where it is made yeasts have built up over the years that give it a unique flavour. The cheese is kept in straw-lined pits from August to November, when celebrations accompany its pungent unearthing.

Caciotta is a cows' milk cheese, usually milder than pecorino. White and crumbly, it is similar to English Cheshire cheese.

For the best cheese, you should buy either from small delicatessens or big supermarkets with dedicated counters. Some delis are designed more for tourists than locals, and quality can suffer. Watch where the locals go, and ask for a taste – a good shop will be happy to oblige.

Meat and fish The wild boar, once an endangered species in the region, has now become a pest in some areas, and even if you don't glimpse them around the wooded hills of the Apennines you will probably see the evidence of their snuffling for food on the ground. Wild boar meat features on many menus, often as sausages, or with *pappardelle* (pasta ribbons). Other cured meats are common too.

Inland, you will probably also come across Chianina beef, from a strain of large white cattle, and freshwater fish. Eel is traditional, as is wood pigeon. On the Marche coast – especially in Ancona and Pesaro – there are some great seafood restaurants, where they serve fish straight off the boats.

Olive oil Some of the best olive oil in Italy is produced in neighbouring Umbria. For the highest quality, look for a fresh, green colour.

The reasons for the high quality of the oil here are mainly climatic. In the foothills of the Apennines, varieties survive that produce less fruit but more flavour. They are, however, also susceptible to the extreme cold weather that is possible here. At well-irrigated, warmer, lower levels, yields are higher but quality may not be so good.

When buying olive oil look for the expiry date, which by Italian law must be two years after it was made. The newer the oil the better – the best time to buy is in November or December when the new pressing has just arrived in the shops.

Wine Marche has 13 DOC wines. Most prominent are whites, especially Verdicchio. There are plenty more varieties to look out for, however, and vineyards are increasingly opening their doors to visitors. Conero wine comes from the hills near Ancona. It is dry and full-bodied and made up of at least 85% Montepulciano grapes and up to 15% Sangiovese.

Eating out

Most restaurants will offer an *antipasto* (a starter), followed by a *primo* (first course, usually pasta) and a *secondo* (second course, usually meat) with *contorni* (side dishes) and a *dolce* (dessert). Don't feel pressured into having everything, however, or even into sticking to the order – nobody will mind if you just have a second course, or a side dish without the meat, or a salad as a first course. And despite the preponderance of meat – often wild boar, Chianina beef or game – it's usually eaten as a separate course, so vegetarians won't have a hard time finding good food.

Pizzerias, often run by Neapolitans and serving excellent pizzas, are common and are often open later than standard restaurants – usually until 2400 or 0100. Most bars also serve food – Italians rarely drink without eating, and *enoteche* (wine bars) can be great places for a light lunch or supper.

Breakfast is usually a *cornetto* (a sweet croissant, often jam- or custard-filled) grabbed at a café or bar. The standard of breakfast in hotels is usually poor, so you might be better skipping it and going to the local café. *Agriturismi* do much better. Locals eat lunch around 1300. Evenings often start with an *aperitivo* around 1900, followed by supper any time from 2000 or 2100 until around 2300.

Festivals in Marche

February

Carnevale Carnival is celebrated everywhere, but nowhere with quite as much gusto as Ascoli Piceno, where masked parades and accompanying parties go on for a week.

July

Sferisterio Opera Festival Macerata, www.sferisterio.it. The strangely wide Sferisterio (see page 52) was built for a now obscure sport, but makes a great open-air setting for Marche's top opera festival, which runs into Aug.

Ancona Jazz www.anconajazz.com. At more or less the same time as Umbria Jazz, this festival takes place on the Adriatic coast.

August

Rossini Opera Festival Pesaro, T072-1380 0294, www.rossinioperafestival.it. Works by Pesaro's favourite son are performed in his hometown.

Ferragosto National holiday on 5 Aug celebrating the harvest and end of hard labour in the fields and the holy day for Assumption of the Blessed Virgin Mary. The entire month is often taken as a holiday with offices, shops and businesses reopening in Sep.

December

Christmas Cribs and nativity scenes spring up everywhere. In Frasassi, along the route to the Tempietto del Valadier (see page 50), there are 'live' Christmas scenes, with costumed locals playing various parts.

Essentials A-Z

Accident and emergency
Ambulance T118; **Fire** T115; **Police** T113 (with English-speaking operators), T112 (*carabinieri*); **Roadside assistance** T116.

Electricity
Italy functions on a 220V mains supply. Plugs are the standard European 2-pin variety.

Health
Comprehensive travel and medical insurance is strongly recommended for all travel. EU citizens should apply for a free European Health Insurance Card (www.ehic.org), which has replaced the E111 form and offers free or reduced-cost medical treatment.

Medical services
Late-night pharmacies are identified by a large green cross outside: call T1100 for addresses of the 3 nearest open pharmacies. The accident and emergency department of a hospital is the *pronto soccorso*.

Language
In hotels and bigger restaurants, you'll usually find English is spoken. The further you go from the tourist centres, however, the more trouble you may have, unless you have at least a smattering of Italian.

Italians from the rest of the country often consider modern-day *Marchigiani* to speak with a rather slow, rural Italian, and though such attitudes are exaggerated, you may be able to detect a country lilt to some spoken language in the region. That said, it's seldom hard to understand.

Marchigiano dialects still exist, especially in rural areas, and sometimes in the names of traditional local dishes. Closely connected to standard Italian, you may notice the occasional dropping of the last syllable, and substitution of 'u' for a final 'o'.

Money → *For exchange rates see www.xe.com.*
The Italian currency is the euro (€). There are ATMs (*bancomat*) throughout Italy that accept major credit and debit cards. To change cash or travellers' cheques throughout Umbria, look for a *cambio*. Many restaurants, shops, museums and art galleries will take major credit cards. Paying directly with debit cards such as Cirrus is less easy in many places, so withdrawing from an ATM and paying in cash may be the better option. Keep some cash for toll roads if you're driving.

Cost of living
Staying in a cheap agriturismo and eating picnics, you could just about get by on €75 a day per person. Double that for a more comfortable holiday, with swimming pool, truffles and Sagrantino.

When visiting tourist attractions you can often buy combined tickets that let you into several sights, though the savings aren't always great. Students and children usually go half price.

Opening hours
Most shops and tourist attractions close at lunchtime. Almost no shops open on Sun and museums are often closed on Mon.

Safety
The crime rate in Italy is generally low, though rates of petty crime are higher. Take care when travelling: don't flaunt your valuables; take only what money you need and split it; don't take risks you wouldn't at home. Beware of scams and con-artists, and don't expect things to go smoothly if you partake in fake goods. Car break-ins are common, so always remove valuables. Take care on public transport, where pickpockets or bag-cutters operate. Earthquakes are a possibility – if you experience one, stay in the open if possible or, if not, shelter in a doorway.

Time
Italy uses Central European Time, GMT+1.

Tipping
Only in the more expensive restaurants will staff necessarily expect a tip, although everyone will be grateful for one; 10-15% is the norm, and it's increasingly common for service to be included in your bill on top of the cover charge. When you're ordering at the bar a few spare coins may speed service up. Taxis may add on extra costs for luggage, but an additional tip is always appreciated. Rounding up prices always goes down well, especially if it means avoiding giving change – not a favourite Italian habit.

Tourist information
Even small towns have tourist information offices, where you can get a map and advice on the best sights. Most also have lists of accommodation. *Agriturismi* (see page 10) are worth booking before you arrive.

In the university towns, look out for student-produced information.

Visas
UK and EU citizens do not need a visa, but will need a valid passport to enter Italy. A standard tourist visa for those outside the EU is valid for up to 90 days.

Contents

Footprint features

Northern Marche

Urbino is one of Italy's most picture-perfect Renaissance towns and has been a great centre of learning and the arts for hundreds of years. The huge Palazzo Ducale dominates the surrounding landscape and the town retains much of its 15th- and 16th-century structure, as well as being home to 21st-century contemporary university life.

Further inland, to the north, the Montefeltro is an isolated area, with craggy outcrops formed into eccentric shapes and topped with castles rising precipitously out of the landscape. San Leo has a spectacularly sited fortress at the top of a cliff, and there are lots of other villages to explore. It is an area of poets and artisans, of beer and cheese, as well as traditional arts.

Just south of here, across the border in Umbria, is the Parco del Monte Cucco, which has some excellent walking, not to mention world-class hang-gliding. On the the western edge of the park, Gubbio has a Roman theatre, an extraordinary medieval town hall and a very special cable car, which whisks passengers two at a time up Monte Ingino in fragile-looking baskets.

Out on the coast, Pesaro and Fano are old-fashioned resorts, but both have good beaches and handsome antique centres to compensate for their garish seafronts. North of Pesaro, where the hills reach right to the sea, Gradara is another castellated town with a tragically romantic past.

Urbino → *For listings, see pages 34-41.*

Hill-town Urbino, birthplace of Raphael and home to spectacular Renaissance architecture and the National Gallery of the Palazzo Ducale, is perhaps Marche's most obvious tourist attraction. It has been a centre of learning and culture since the Renaissance: its university was founded in 1507, and Pope Clement XI was born here in 1700. Today, students outnumber other inhabitants in a town where many of the symbols of Urbino's apogee of influence and power in the 15th century remain in place.

Arriving in Urbino

Getting there and around Urbino isn't accessible by train; the nearest stations are Pesaro or Fano. There are seven daily buses from Pesaro (90 minutes), which arrive at the bus station in the piazza Mercatale (T0722-2196); buses run from here into the centre.

From the main car park at piazza Mercatale, steep steps or a lift take you up into *centro storico*.

Tourist information Tourist information office ① *via Puccinotti 33, T0722-320437, www. urbinoeilmontefeltro.it*. For €10, the *biglietto unico* admits you to all of Urbino's main sights.

Palazzo Ducale

① *Piazza Duca Federico, T0722-322625, www.galleriaborghese.it. Mon 0830-1400 (last entry 1230), Tue-Sun 0830-1915 (last entry 1800), €5, concession €2.50, EU citizens under 18s and over 65s free.*

The huge palace built by Federico da Montefelcro and his wife Battista Sforza dominates the town. Work on it started in 1465, at a time when the court was a reference point for the Italian Renaissance. Architect Luciano Laurana took charge of the project, though Piero della Francesca was also involved and Battista Sforza herself was instrumental in incorporating Renaissance theories about the links between culture and design into the structure. When she died in 1472, at the age of 26, Laurana left, and the nature of the construction changed, with Renaissance thought taking a less prominent role. As a result, the later rooms are less vibrant, their purpose often less clear.

The entrance to the palace takes you straight into the **Cortile d'Onore**, a large, elegant, porticoed courtyard. Brick and stone are used to create patterns, and engraved lettering along the cornice reads: "Federico, Duke of Urbino, Count of Montefeltro and Casteldurante, Knight of the Holy Roman Church and Commander of the Italic Confederation built this house, raised from its foundations to celebrate his glory and that of posterity," before going on to detail his military successes.

Just off the courtyard, in a position of unusual prominence, the Duke's library is, these days, bereft of books, though a colourful projection scrolling on to the walls effectively demonstrates the ornateness of the manuscripts that once lined the room. The books themselves are now held in the Vatican Library.

Downstairs, to the right of the entrance, is the area that once held the practical workings of the palace – the kitchens and washrooms, wine cellars and ice-rooms. The intelligent design of the building can also be seen here, with pipes that carried hot water and ventilation as well as drainage.

The palace's most obvious attractions are upstairs, however, where the paintings of the **National Gallery of the Marche** are exhibited. Highlights include Piero della Francesca's poised *Madonna di Senigallia* and his *Flagellation of Christ*; a famous, but unattributed,

Urbino's golden age

The settlement of Urvinum Mataurense became a Roman municipality in the third century BC. For hundreds of years it held an important strategic position, though its golden age was not until the 15th century, by which time it had been under the control of the Montefeltro family for two centuries. When Oddantonio da Montefeltro became Duke of Urbino in 1443, aged just 16, he was more interested in owning fast horses than looking after his territories, and after a year of misrule he was thrown to his death from a window of his palace by an angry mob. Federico, his illegitimate half-brother, took over and began to build bridges.

By the time he married his second wife, the 14-year-old Battista Sforza, in 1460, Federico had already gained a reputation as a wise ruler. Over the 12 years of their marriage, Urbino became a focal point for the Renaissance, and

Piero della Francesca was among those who came to work at the ducal court.

After the death of Federico's son and heir in 1508, the influence and importance of Urbino began slowly to ebb away. In 1523 the court moved to Pesaro, and in 1631 the last duke died. The estate passed to the papacy, and the Palazzo Ducale was emptied of many of its treasures. At the same time, a generous dowry for the marriage of Vittoria della Rovere into the Florentine Medici family, reputedly to compensate for her 'awkwardness', meant that the city lost even more of its artistic patrimony.

In 1700, Urbino-born Giovanni Albani became Pope Clement XI and reversed some of the city's decline, but, though it continued to be one of Italy's most important centres of learning, its days at the centre of Italian influence were long gone.

painting of the *Ideal City*, from around 1470, which demonstrates great skill in the use of perspective; Giovanni Bellini's *Sacra Conversazione*; and, best of all, Raphael's *La Muta*, or *Portrait of a Gentlewoman*, an enigmatic and intriguing portrait. Other notable works include Paolo Uccello's *Miracle of the Desecrated Host* (1465-1469) – a six-panel storyboard, painted for the predella of an altarpiece, illustrating the story of a Parisian Jew burned at the stake for having profaned the host.

Also on this floor is the apartment of the duke himself, including the spectacular alcove bedstead – a sort of wooden box, painted and with lots of wood embossing – in which he slept. The room still referred to in some places as the *Sala degli Uomini d'Arme* ('room of the men-at-arms') has now been renamed the **Sala delle Nozze di Federico**, after a restoration uncovered fragments of murals that include Battista Sforza's coat of arms (a lion and a quince tree) showing that the room was probably decorated for the marriage of Federico and Battista.

Don't miss Federico's **studiolo**, a small room panelled with extraordinary works of intarsia (inlaid wood), illustrating symbols of learning – mathematics, music, astronomy and the fine arts – with exceptional three-dimensionality.

The third floor of the palace opens only for 20 minutes every hour, on the hour, which is probably enough. Compared to the masterpieces on the second floor, much of the art here seems hackneyed and there is an excess of soft-focus, rosy-cheeked 17th-century ephemera, though there are some notable exceptions, such as Sassoferrato's three-panelled *Annunciation, Adoration and Circumcision*, which stands out for its use of colour and well-observed detail, and an exquisite 16th-century ebony chest, inlaid with ivory.

Back on the ground floor, the archaeological section of ancient inscriptions in stone is only of passing interest, but there's a café and a shop, should you be in need of retail or caffeine therapy.

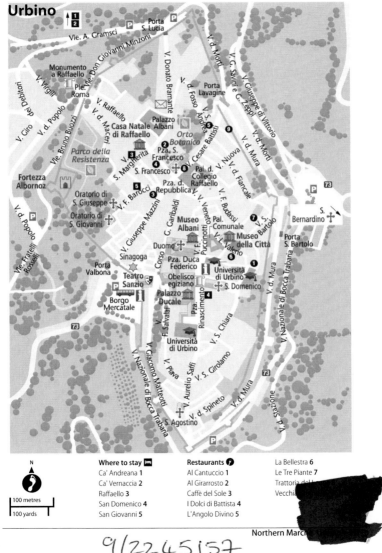

Urbino

9/2245157

Where to stay 🛏
Ca' Andreana **1**
Ca' Vernaccia **2**
Raffaello **3**
San Domenico **4**
San Giovanni **5**

Restaurants ❼
Al Cantuccio **1**
Al Girarrosto **2**
Caffè del Sole **3**
I Dolci di Battista **4**
L'Angolo Divino **5**

La Bellestra **6**
Le Tre Piante **7**
Trattoria del
Vecchia

N
100 metres
100 yards

Duomo

① *Piazza Duca Federico. Daily 0730-1300, 1400-2000, free.*

In 1781 an earthquake damaged Urbino's cathedral, and after eight years of restoration the entire dome collapsed down into the cathedral below. Subsequent reconstruction has left a building that is more impressive in size than in beauty, though two chapels, at either side of the apse, survive from earlier times and are worth a look for their ornate detailing. The right-hand **Cappella della Concezione** has a fragment of 14th-century fresco of the *Madonna and Child* over the altar.

Casa Natale di Raffaello

① *Via Raffaello 57, T0722-320105, www.accademiaraffaello.it. Mar-Oct Mon-Sat 0900-1300 and 1500-1900, Sun 1000-1300, Nov-Feb Mon-Sat 0900-1400, Sun 1000-1300, €3.*

Raffaello Sanzio was born in Urbino on 28 March 1483, and his house, just up the hill from the piazza, can be visited. He was the son of a well-known painter, Giovanni Santi, who died when Raphael was 11; his mother died soon after he was born. The one original painting here by Raphael is an early fresco, originally thought to be by his father.

Oratorio de San Giovanni and Oratorio di San Giuseppe

① *Via Barocci, T347-671 1181 (mobile). Mon-Sat 1000-1230, 1500-1730, Sun 1000-1230, €2.50 and €2 respectively.*

These two small neighbouring churches both have artistic claims to fame. The Oratorio di San Giovanni is especially spectacular, the interior being richly decorated with mostly intact frescoes illustrating the life of St John the Baptist. Look for the small dog present in many of the images. Painted by brothers Jacopo and Lorenzo Salimbeni in 1416, the images are great examples of a style known as 'flamboyant Gothic'.

On the right-hand wall as you face the altar, nine panels cover St John's birth, his meeting with Mary, his baptism of Jesus and his preaching to the masses. On the wall behind the altar is an extraordinarily complex and inventive Crucifixion, while on the left wall John appears twice with no head. The figure in the black cloak here is Pietro Spagnolo, a much-respected Urbino hermit whose body now lies below the altar.

The Oratorio di San Giuseppe is less remarkable, though it contains Federico Brandani's lugubrious life-sized Nativity scene in a specially built grotto. The main room, a high-ceilinged vaulted space, is also worth a look for its floor-to-ceiling decoration.

Fortezza Albornoz

① *Park open daily 0900-1900, free.*

Though you can't enter the fortress itself, Urbino's castle grounds are a popular spot for the view they give back over the town, especially at sunset, when you'll probably find pairs of lovers lolling under every apple tree.

Orto Botanico

① *Via Donato Bramante 28, T0722-303774. Mon-Wed and Fri, 0800-1230, 1500-1730, free.*

A peaceful and serious garden, Urbino University's collection of plants is a shady place, where occasional dappled beams of sunshine make it down through the trees to the flowers and plants below. An information board explains the relationship of the areas of the garden to parts of the body, but most visitors are happy just to wander in and out of walled rows of plants, all hand labelled in Latin.

Museo della Citta
ⓘ *Palazzo Odasi, via Valerio 1, T0722-309270, www.museodelmetauro.it. Wed-Mon 1000-1300, 1500-1800, free.*

Urbino's town museum, in the Palazzo Odasi, is influenced by Calvino's **Invisible Cities** (as Calvino was influenced by Urbino). It is designed to "contain ideas rather than objects" and is part contemporary art, part conventional museum. Traces of Roman architecture can be seen under glass in the courtyard and there are rooms on engraved signs, book decoration and "the city and desire".

Around Urbino → *For listings, see pages 34-41.*

Gola del Furlo

A 20-minute drive southwest of Urbino, the Furlo Gorge is a spectacular ravine cut precipitously through the Apennine Mountains by the green, meandering river Candigliano. This east–west route was the narrowest pass of the via Flaminia – one of ancient Rome's most important roads.

The gorge was also a favourite spot of Mussolini, and he had an enormous profile of his face built at the top of the towering cliff on the gorge's northern side. Best seen from the village of Furlo itself, Il Duce's face is still recognizable, despite having being blown up by partisans.

On the wooded slopes above the gorge there are good walks, and the chance to stop and picnic on **Mussolini's broken nose**. The easiest approachis a 90-minute walk from Pagino, a tiny hamlet northwest of Furlo, where there is parking next to a church. From here, follow the track between fields, branching left at a shrine, which becomes a stony path after about 15 minutes. Keep right at a fork in the path by a tall tree after another 10 minutes and climb for another 45 minutes or so through pine and cedar trees until you reach a dog-leg left just before a red and white barrier. Ten minutes along this grassier path brings you out to a clearing at the top of the hill. Turn left here on to a path that shortly emerges on to the rocky upturned face of the fascist dictator, with stunning views east to the Adriatic, west to the Apennines and vertiginously down to the green waters swirling through the gorge far, far below.

San Leo and Montefeltro → *For listings, see pages 34-41.*

Tucked into the northern corner of Marche, Montefeltro is a strange, half-forgotten landscape of rocky outcrops, sheer cliffs and rolling green hills – a sort of central Italian Middle-earth. San Leo is the area's most obvious attraction – a town with a Renaissance castle that towers over it on the sheer cliff above, with views to the tiny republic of San Marino. There are other highlights though, such as the little-known Parco Naturale Sasso Simone e Simoncello, and a big landscape full of little treats such as the Garden of Forgotten Fruit and Pietrarubbia, an isolated hamlet in the hills, rich in art and museums.

Arriving in San Leo
Getting there and around In summer (June to September) there are two direct buses a day from Rimini to San Leo; at other times it's necessary to change at Pietracuta. There's no public transport on Sundays. For the rest of the area a car is pretty much essential.

San Leo itself is tiny, but if you don't fancy a bit of a climb you might want to catch the bus or a taxi up the hill to the castle.

Tourist information Tourist information office ⓘ *Palazzo Mediceo, piazza Dante Alighieri 14, T0541-916306, www.san-leo.it, 0900-1900.*

La Fortezza
ⓘ *Mar-Oct daily 0900-1900, winter hours vary, €8 or €10 combined ticket with Torre Campanaria and Museo d'Arte Sacra.*

San Leo's castle is the epitome of imposing, built as an extension of a precipitous rock face jutting out of the Marecchia Valley. It is an obvious place for a fortress, and indeed there has been one here since the sixth century, and perhaps as far back as Roman times. From the 17th to the early 20th century it was used as a prison and, despite its elegance, it remains a formidable building, with little of the fairytale castle romance of Gradara. Much of the design seen today is the work of Renaissance architect Francesco di Giorgio Martini, who reinforced and enhanced the existing structure for Federico da Montefeltro in the 15th century. Having captured the castle in 1441, Federico's enhancements strengthened it against cannon fire and made it more or less impenetrable. The castle contains a small museum of weapons and armour, a torture chamber and various cells where unfortunate prisoners spent their last days.

The *fortezza* is a five-minute walk uphill through woods from the village below, or there's a car park just outside the walls.

Palazzo Mediceo e Museo d'Arte Sacra
ⓘ *Daily 0900-1900, though hours may vary, €8 or €10 combined ticket with Fortezza and Torre Campanaria.*

In the centre of San Leo, the Palazzo Mediceo houses the tourist information office as well as a small museum of sacred art. Luca Frosino's Botticelliesque *Madonna and Child* (1487-1493) shows the Virgin flanked by local saints Leo and Marino.

Duomo di San Leone
ⓘ *Daily 1000-1900, free.*

Construction of San Leo's cathedral, a fine Romanesque building, was completed in 1173. The raised presbytery is a handsome feature, as are the high Romanesque arches. Built from pale sandstone, it has a well-worn but dignified feel. Look for Roman columns and carved capitals used in the building.

Behind the *duomo* is the **Torre Campanaria** ⓘ *daily 1000-1200, 1500-1900*, also 12th century: a square bell tower built straight on to a rocky outcrop.

Pieve di Santa Maria Assunta
ⓘ *Daily 1000-1900, free.*

A bare stone building with plenty of atmosphere, this ancient church was probably first erected in the eighth century and rebuilt in the 11th, though the crypt downstairs may be an even earlier chapel where the fourth-century St Leo used to pray. Ancient Roman elements, such as capitals at the top of columns, were used in the church's construction. The elegant stone canopy over the altar is from the ninth century.

Parco Naturale Sasso Simone e Simoncello
ⓘ *www.parcosimone.it.*

The hills of this little-known regional park have rocky plateaux and woods of oak and beech trees, maple and hornbeam. Owls, buzzards, kestrels and peregrine falcons patrol the skies, while down below deer, porcupines and wolves roam. The park covers nearly 5000 ha and rises to 1415 m at the summit of **Monte Carpegna**, the watershed between the Foglia and Marecchia valleys. There is a visitor centre near Pietrarubbia at **Ponte Cappuccini** ① *via Montefeltresca, T0722-75350, Mon-Fri 0900-1300, Sat 1000-1200, Sun 0900-1200*, and local tourist information offices can also provide maps of walking and cycling routes.

Castello di Pietrarubbia
① *T0722-750031, www.comune.pietrarubbia.pu.it.*
Until recently a ruined hamlet, complete with its own little castle on top of the hill, Pietrarubbia has some of the best views in central Italy, across a wide expanse of rolling countryside to the high hills of the Parco Naturale Sasso Simone e Simoncello, as well as to San Leo and San Marino.

The entire place has now been taken over by an association and is run with enormous enthusiasm as a restaurant, hotel (see page 35), museums, art complex and open-air gallery. The **sculpture museum** (variable hours – ask at the hotel or restaurant if it's closed), in a great space overlooking the hills, exhibits some interesting work from the art school that is based here. Other, larger pieces are scattered around the village, some of them by Italian sculptor Arnaldo Pomodoro, turning the whole place into a contemporary sculpture park. There's also an interesting museum of ceramics that were found during the restoration of the village.

A path leads up between wild roses from the far end of the village to a restored lookout tower at the top of the hill, from where the views are fantastic.

L'Orto dei Frutti Dimenticati
① *Pennabilli, www.montefeltro.net/pennabilli. Daily 0900-1900, free, guided tours on request from the tourist office (T0541-928659).*
One of seven open-air museums in and around Pennabilli, grouped together as **I Luoghi dell'Anima**, the Garden of Forgotten Fruit is both a serious attempt to preserve ancient species of fruit trees and a sculpture garden with a view. It's also a good reason to call in on the pleasant hill town of **Pennabilli**, home to Italian poet and screenwriter Tonino Guerra, many of whose projects enliven the cultural life of the area. Other places include Il Santuario dei Pensieri, the Sanctuary of Thoughts.

Parco Regionale di Monte Cucco → *For listings, see pages 34-41.*

① *Park authority: Consorzio Obbligatorio di Gestione del Parco del Monte Cucco Villa Anita, via Matteotti 52, Sigillo, T075-917 7326, www.parcomontecucco.it.*
Southwest of the Gola del Furlo, on the border with Umbria, the Apennines rise high above the valley floor, and the beech forests on their flanks are home to wild boar, wolves, wild cats, golden eagles and porcupines. A protected area, on the Umbrian side of the border, surrounds the peaks, culminating at the top of Monte Cucco, 1566 m above sea level. Below ground, the park has a huge cave system, descending over 990 m, while above is a favourite spot for paragliders and hang-gliders – the 2008 Women's Hang-gliding World Championships were held here.

There are some great walks to be done, notably to the summit of Monte Cucco but also in the **Rio Freddo Gorge** and in more remote valleys such as the **Valle delle Prigioni**. In winter, attention switches to cross-country skiing.

Monte Cucco

The easiest approach to Monte Cucco is up via del Ranco from the village of Sigillo. After several vertiginous switchbacks this forks left to **Pian di Monte** and right to the small hamlet of **Ranco**. In summer a couple of bars and restaurants open here, and many Italians set up weekend picnics on the grassy slopes beside the road.

Well-signposted paths lead from the car park below the **Albergo Ristorante Monte Cucco di Tobia** ① *T075-917 7194, www.albergomontecucco.it*, out into the beech forest. Even in high summer the crowds of Val di Ranco soon disappear, and the only sounds are the breeze in the trees and a chorus of crickets in the clearings.

To the summit A good, four-hour circular walk from Val di Ranco, via the summit of Monte Cucco, initially follows *sentiero 1* from the car park in front of the restaurant. Marked with red-and-white striped waymarks, as well as occasional signposts, the wide, easy path curves around through the trees before bearing right by a spring and, after about 45 minutes, climbing steeply through the **Passo del Lupo**. The forest here is especially beautiful, with sunlight filtering down through mature trees and a scattering of flowers on the forest floor. Cowbells signal the whereabouts of grazing herds. A half-hour ascent brings you out at a refuge, with good views and a large area of grass – another popular summer picnic spot.

From here a road heads north – go along it for 150 m or so, until a path (*sentiero 2*) leads off to the left. This is an especially steep climb, but well worth it for what awaits above the tree line. Turn left to follow a blessedly flat, well-constructed path along the edge of steep slopes covered with grass and orchids. The path becomes increasingly spectacular as it bends around the mountain. At the next junction, turn right on to *sentiero 14*, which leads to the summit of the mountain, with breathtaking views in all directions.

Below the summit to the south, a path back down to Pian di Monte winds east from an iron cross. You'll probably see hang-gliders and paragliders. From here you can follow the road back to Val di Ranco.

Gubbio → *For listings, see pages 34-41.*

West of the Parco Regionale del Monte Cucco, on the Umbrian side of the Appennine Mountains, traditional Gubbio retains its medieval feel, with pale grey stone arched streets and keenly held loyalties to the four ancient quarters of the city. Its central piazza is a spectacular and ambitious ensemble of Gothic architecture, and there are several worthwhile sights, including the cathedral, several churches and palazzi, and an adrenaline-inducing cable car ride to the top of Monte Ingino.

Probably the central settlement of the pre-Roman Umbri people, Gubbio is proud of its roots, and the museum houses the Eugubian Tablets, vital to the understanding of the linguistic and cultural history of Italy. The ruins of a Roman theatre sit outside the old city walls, and several enthusiastically enacted festivals and palios through the year underline the town's fascination with the past.

Even in high summer Gubbio rarely feels overrun with visitors. Contrasting with some industrial development in the plain below the town, the high hills rising to the east, which culminate in the Parco Regionale del Monte Cucco, are a cool escape into the high Umbrian wilderness.

Arriving in Gubbio

Getting there and around Not on the train line, Gubbio is served by regular buses from Perugia (40 km). The nearest station is 19 km away at Fossato di Vico on the Rome–Ancona line. It's a 30-minute bus journey into Gubbio. Walking is the easiest way to get around the town. There's free parking near the Teatro Romano. Buses arrive at and leave from piazza Quaranta Martiri, and run from here to the cable car station and most main sites.

Tourist information Tourist information office ① *via della Repubblica 15, T075-922 0693, www.comune.gubbio.pg.it, Mon-Fri 0830-1345, 1530-1830, Sat 0900-1300, 1530-1830, Sun 0930-1230, 1530-1830 (Oct-Mar afternoons 1500-1800).*

Piazza Grande

At the centre of the four quarters of the medieval town, Gubbio's 14th-century piazza was built as a unifying point, as well as to emphasize the power of the State over the Church following the construction of the Duomo, just up the hill. The building of the piazza was agreed in 1322, but it was not finished until 1483.

Despite the gigantic Palazzo dei Consoli, it is not until it is seen from below, along via Ubaldo Baldassini, that the extraordinary scale of the project becomes clear. The piazza is raised on four huge stone arches, each the size of a small house, in order to create a large flat area on the Gubbio slopes.

Facing the Palazzo dei Consoli is the **Palazzo del Podestà**, built to a similar design, but unfinished and nowadays used for temporary exhibitions.

Palazzo dei Consoli

① *Piazza Grande, T075-927 4298, www.comune.gubbio.pg.it. Apr-Oct 1000-1300, 1500-1800, Nov-Mar 1000-1300, 1400-1700, €5.*

Containing the **Museo Civico** as well as the art gallery and the archaeological museum, the 60-m-tall Palazzo dei Consoli towers over the town. Though the stars of the show are the famous **Tavole Iguvine** – also known as the Eugubian or Eugubine Tablets – other attractions include fantastic views from the top of the tower, some good Gothic art and even some medieval toilets.

Steps from piazza Grande rise to the main entrance and the huge, barrel-vaulted **Sala d'Arengo** (Assembly Room), which is now home to various fragments of stone from Umbri and Roman times, from gravestones to engraved signs from the ancient theatre. Downstairs, the new oriental and Risorgimento collections are generally of less interest, though there are some impressive pieces of Tibetan metalwork.

On the first floor are the Eugubian Tablets: seven large bronze plates engraved with text, five in Umbrian, two in Latin. Often compared to the Rosetta Stone, they describe rites and religious ceremonies, including animal sacrifices intended to protect the city from its enemies. They are important because of what they have taught scholars about pre-Roman times and language, but are also beautiful objects in their own right, with text that seems remarkably modern in both style and execution. Occasional mistakes give them an extra human angle.

There is some debate about how they were discovered, but the most common story is that in 1444 they were found by a farmer in an underground chamber near the Roman theatre, and that he sold them to the city in 1456 in return for two years' grazing rights.

Look for the palazzo's '*passaggio segreto*' in order to find the medieval toilets ('Don't lift the lid,' a sign declares, ominously), complete with plumbing but without much in the way of privacy.

From here stairs rise to the **Pinacoteca**, on the top floor. The history of Gubbian art is illustrated by paintings such as a rather beautiful 16th-century *Noli me Tangere* on wood, by either Girolamo Genga or Timoteo Viti – as well as the obligatory, and unusually seductive, central Italian landscape, it incorporates a small cupboard for religious relics. Other works to look out for include a *Virgin and Child* by Guiduccio Palmerucci, with local saint Ubaldo featuring prominently. The influence of Sienese art can easily be seen here, in both the profusion of gold and the tender relationship between mother and baby.

From the picture gallery, the **Loggia Panoramica** shouldn't be missed – it has great views over the town and the surrounding countryside.

In the basement, entered from the back of the palazzo, the archaeological museum (same ticket and opening hours) is, by Italian standards, not very exciting, though there are a couple of interesting pieces, including some engraved slingshot and a beautiful eighth-century stone sarcophagus.

Palazzo Ducale

ⓘ *Via della Cattedrale, T075-927 5872, Tue-Sun 0830-1900, €2, under 17s free.*

Gubbio's Ducal Palace, opposite the cathedral, was probably designed by the same architect as the more famous palace in Urbino (see page 19), of which it is a smaller version. The seat of Duke Federico of Montefeltro when he was in town, it was built in the 1470s on the site of a Lombard building. These days the interior is fairly plain, but there is a fine porticoed Renaissance courtyard, as well as some great views across Gubbio.

Duomo

ⓘ *Via Cattedrale, daily 0900-1800, free.*

Up the hill in a quiet part of town, Gubbio's cathedral has an unusual wagon-vaulted ceiling, with small side chapels off a single nave. It was probably designed by Giovanni da Gubbio, who also designed Assisi's cathedral. The building was finished around 1203.

The 1549 choir is impressively carved but inaccessible. There are fragments of original frescoes on the walls, two saints – Giovanni da Lodi and Virginia – and two other holy corpses. The many paintings around the walls include a 16th-century *Pietà* by Dono Doni. A coin machine illuminates the apse and chapel.

Museo Diocesano

ⓘ *Via Federico da Montefeltro, T075-922 0904, www.museogubbio.it, summer 1000-1900, winter 1000-1800 (may close Tue), €4.*

Gubbio's diocesan museum has a good archaeological collection as well as religious paintings. Highlights include fifth- and fourth-century BC pottery and ex-votos, such as a rather surprised-looking donkey carrying two pots and some intricately painted cups. Downstairs, in Mello da Gubbio's 14th-century *Virgin and Child*, some pretty angels surround two decidedly chubby central figures. One of the most impressive objects in the museum can be seen only from the street outside – the *botte grande* is a gargantuan wine barrel from the 15th century, which once held 20,000 litres of wine.

Fontana dei Pazzi

Local myth states that three turns around this fountain, at the northern end of via dei Consoli, will make you mad. There may be a connection with stories that ancient Rome used to send people it considered mad to Gubbio.

Piazza Quaranta Martiri

This large, busy piazza at the bottom of town is the arrival point for buses. Opposite the large Church of San Francesco, the loggia, built in 1603 on top of a 14th-century portico, was once used for the stretching of wool. Nowadays fruit and veg are sold under the awnings, and there's a fully fledged market in the piazza on Tuesday mornings.

The piazza is named after the 40 townsfolk executed here by German soldiers in 1944, in retribution for partisan fighting in the hills. To its south, along via Perugina, a mausoleum commemorates those killed. Behind a flowerbed, bullet holes are still obvious in the wall.

Chiesa di San Francesco

① *Piazza Quaranta Martiri, daily 0715-1200, 1530-1930, free.*

Built in 1256, soon after St Francis's canonization, this pale stone Gothic church has three naves and an attractive cloister, the Chiostro della Pace. In the left apse, early 15th-century frescoes by Ottaviano Nelli tell the story of the *Life of the Virgin*.

Teatro Romano

① *Viale Teatro Romano, daily Apr-Sep 0830-1930, Oct-Mar 0830-1730, free.*

Built some time between 55 and 27 BC, Gubbio's theatre, outside the city walls, may once have held as many as 16,000 spectators, making it one of the biggest Roman theatres. These days it's an evocative, dusty place, with grass growing up between the old stones. Some of its outer arches are still intact, and enough of the central seating survives to make it a good venue for open-air plays in summer.

An antiquarium displays pottery and other Roman remnants found in the area. Also nearby is a ruined Roman mausoleum – the original outer layer is gone, but a 6-m by 4.5-m burial chamber is intact.

Funivia and Basilica di Sant'Ubaldo

① *Cable car: via San Girolamo, T075-927 7507, Mar Mon-Sat 1000-1315, 1430-1730, Sun 0930-1315, 1430-1800; Apr-May Mon-Sat 1000-1315, 1430-1830, Sun 0930-1315, 1430-1800; Jun Mon-Sat 0930-1315, 1430-1900, Sun 0900-1930; Jul-Aug 0900-2000; 1-11 Sep Mon-Sat 0930-1900, Sun 0930-1930; 12-30 Sep Mon-Sat 0930-1900, Sun 0900-1930; Oct 1000-1315, 1430-1800; Nov-Feb Thu-Tue 1000-1315, 1430-1700; €5 return.*

Gubbio's biggest thrill is its eccentric **cable car** ride up Monte Ingino. The five-minute ride to the top, in small baskets that hold two standing passengers, gives extraordinary views of the plain below as you are whisked over the treetops. Getting in and out of the moving, creaking cages is part of the adventure – someone will tell you to stand on a red spot and bundle you in; someone else drags you out at the other end. Hold tight and have your camera well strapped to your wrist.

At the top is a café, a restaurant and the Basilica di Sant'Ubaldo, patron saint of Gubbio. This church is the destination for the annual palio known as the **Corsa dei Ceri**, when the three guilds of Gubbio race against each other, with each team carrying one of the enormous *ceri* – huge wooden 'candles' each weighing around 280 kg. The *ceri* are kept here in the church for the rest of the year.

The basilica is not quite at the top of the hill – from it a path leads up to the **Rocca**, the ruins of an old castle at the summit. The scaffolding just below it is here to support the star of an enormous Christmas 'tree', made of lights, which illuminates the entire hill in December. If one trip in a basket is enough for you, from here you can continue walking north and then east, around to the summit of **Monte Ansciano**, before descending via the **Monastero di San Girolamo** to Gubbio.

Pesaro → *For listings, see pages 34-41.*

With a smattering of art nouveau architecture and the birthplace of composer Rossini among its sights, Pesaro is a Marche seaside resort with an attractive *centro storico*, some good high-end shopping, a rather dated seafront and a good beach. The Romans founded the town as Pisaurum, in the territory of the Piceni, in 184 BC. On the via Flaminia, it was an important trading post. Pesaro's heyday was in the 16th century, when the della Rovere family moved their court here from Urbino.

Arriving in Pesaro
Getting there and around Pasaro is on the coastal Rimini–Rome train line, with frequent trains in both directions. The train station is on the southern edge of the *centro storico*. **Antulinee Bucci** ① *www.autolineebucci.com*, runs buses every half an hour from Fano to Pesaro. There are usually two buses an hour from Urbino – one fast (45 minutes) one slow (75 minutes). The centre of Pesaro itself is small and easily walkable.

Tourist information Tourist information office ① *viale Trieste 164, T0721-69341*. There's also a regional tourist information office opposite the Casa Rossini.

Piazza del Popolo
The arched building on the western side of Pesaro's main piazza is the 15th-century **Palazzo Ducale**. If you ask the gateman he will probably let you in to look at the courtyard. The fountain in the middle of the piazza was built in 1593.

Musei Civici
① *Piazza Toschi Mosca 29, T0721-387541, www.museicivicipesaro.it. Jul-Aug Wed and Fri-Sun 0930-1230, 1600-1900, Tue and Thu 0930-1230, 1600-2230; Sep-Jun Tue-Wed 0930-1230, Thu-Sun 0930-1230, 1600-1900. €4, concession €2, or €7/3 combined ticket with Casa Rossini, free under 14. Free entry 3rd Sun of month.*
Comprising Pesaro's art gallery and ceramics museums, the Palazzo Toschi Mosca contains a large maiolica collection, together with some colourful and mildly interesting pieces from the 16th-century Duchy of Urbino – the duke and his wife can be seen in unforgiving profile in stone at the top of the stairs. Highlights of the art gallery are a little thin on the ground, though Giovanni Bellini's Renaissance altarpiece of the *Coronation of the Virgin* is an impressive work. On the stairs, garnering many second glances, Francesco Nonni's 1939 life-sized ceramic *Salome*, severed head in hand, is depicted as a sleek nude.

Casa Rossini
① *Via Rossini 34, T0721-387357. Jul-Aug Wed and Fri-Sun 0930-1230, 1600-1900, Tue and Thu 0930-1230, 1600-2230; Sep-Jun Tue-Wed 0930-1230, Thu-Sun 0930-1230, 1600-1900. €4, concession €2, free under 14.*
Gioacchino Rossini, composer of *The Barber of Seville* and many other operas, was born here in 1792. The house was declared a national monument in 1904 and these days contains a collection of prints of Rossini and his contemporaries. In the cellar, Rossini operas play on

---

a constant loop, though the sound quality is poor. Beyond the historical curiosity there's little to detain visitors for very long.

Cattedrale
ⓘ *Via Rossini, T0721-30043.*
The most interesting parts of the cathedral are the mosaics found underneath the floor. On two levels, they were uncovered in the 19th century and date from the sixth and fourth centuries respectively. Glass panels allow visitors to look down on fragments of the 600 sq m of what was probably the floor of an early Christian basilica. The Romanesque façade of the cathedral survived a 19th-century renovation that left little else of beauty.

Opposite, the **Museo Diocesano** ⓘ *T0721-371219, Tue and Sat-Sun 1600-2000, Wed-Fri 1700-2230, €3,* has archaeological and art sections.

Biblioteca and Museo Oliveriano
ⓘ *Palazzo Almerici, via Mazza 97, T0721-33344. Library Mon-Fri 0830-1330, 1430-1845; museum Jul-Aug 1600-1900, Sep-Jun 0900-1200; free. Outside of Jul-Aug, ask upstairs at the library, and somebody will open the museum for you.*
Superior Pesaro's more obvious sights are the library and museum in the Palazzo Almerici. The archaeological museum has finds from the Picene necropolis at Novilara, south of Pesaro – oil lamps and coins among its collection – while upstairs the working library has some beautiful illuminated manuscripts, including a Neapolitan book of hours from 1625 and a 1767 encyclopaedia of science that explains in meticulous detail how to make cannon balls. Ask to see the **Sala Manoscritti**, which has a fascinating map from 1508-1510 showing the first sketchy concept of the Americas.

Around Pesaro → *For listings, see pages 34-41.*

To the immediate north of Pesaro, the natural park of Monte San Bartolo rises out of the sea. Beyond is the romantic walled town and castle of Gradara, at Marche's most northerly point.

Parco Naturale del Monte San Bartolo
ⓘ *www.parks.it/parco.monte.san.bartolo.*
A little like the better-known Parco del Conero further south, San Bartolo is a rare stretch of the Adriatic coast where hills reach to the sea, preventing the development that has blighted much of the coastline. And while it is hardly a wilderness, its rural nature means it is a relatively peaceful area, and a good place for walking – ask for a map at the tourist information office in Pesaro or Fano. The website has information on places to stay in the park.

Gradara
ⓘ *Tourist information office: via delle Mura 4, T0541-964673, www.gradarainnova.it. Jun-Aug daily 0900-1300, 1500-2300; Sep-May Mon-Sat 0900-1300, 1400-1800, Sun 1000-1300, 1400-1800.*
Construction started around 1150 on this impressive castle and walled town, one of the most intact medieval structures in Italy. Lucrezia Borgia lived here for a while and it was the setting for one of Italy's most famous love stories: the tragedy of Francesca and Paolo (see box, page 32).

From the entrance to the medieval town at the **Torre del Orologio** it's possible to walk a good stretch of the walls along the **Camminamenti di Ronda** ⓘ *Jun-Aug 1000-1300*

Francesca and Paolo

The story of Francesca and Paolo has been immortalized in verse by Dante in the *Divine Comedy* and in stone by Rodin with *The Kiss*, put to music by Rachmaninov and painted by Ingres.

The beautiful Francesca da Rimini, daughter of the Lord of Ravenna, was married off by her father to Gianciotto, son of the Lord of Gradara, around 1275. It was a marriage designed to seal the peace between the two families, who had previously been at war. Paolo, the younger and, by all accounts, more attractive brother of Gianciotto, was sent to marry Francesca by proxy. Apparently it was not until the day after the wedding that Francesca realized whom she had really married.

Gianciotto spent much of his time in Pesaro, leaving his wife alone in Gradara castle. Paolo took to visiting Francesca and the two read together, including the story of Lancelot and Guinevere. They became lovers but were caught by Gianciotto, who killed them both with his sword. Dante, their contemporary, placed the pair in the Circle of Lust in his *Inferno*.

and 1400-2300, Sep-May 0900-1300, 1430-1830, €2, and also climb to the top of one of the town's 17 towers.

The **Rocca** ① *www.castellodigradara.com*, Mon 0830-1315, Tue-Sun 0830-1830, also evenings in Jul-Aug, €4, concession €2, lovingly restored in the 20th century, is an atmospheric place. The epitome of most castle fantasies, it has red-draped four-poster beds, frescoed walls, beautiful heavy furniture and long dining rooms. There are a few worthwhile paintings, such as a *Madonna Enthroned* by Giovanni Santi, father of Raphael. Don't miss the barrel-vaulted chapel on the ground floor, with an altarpiece by Andrea della Robbia.

Fano → For listings, see pages 34-41.

Just down the coast from Pesaro, Fano is a smaller resort that doubles as a fishing town, with a Roman arch leading to a compact *centro storico*. The town has an unexpectedly young vibe, with bookshops and clothes shops as well as pensioners on bikes. There are two good beaches: the smaller, sandy **Spiaggia Lido** and the longer, pebbly, **Spiaggia Sassonia**. Between the two is the fishing port, adding a working feel to the town, as well as some excellent fish restaurants.

Arriving in Fano

Fano's train station is on the main Rimini–Rome line, with frequent trains in both directions. **Autolinee Bucci** ① *www.autolineebucci.com*, runs buses every half an hour from Pesaro, and less frequently from Urbino.

Piazza XX Settembre

On Fano's central piazza, the **Palazzo del Podestà**, next to the tower, dates from 1299 and was the seat of power in the area. It was first used as a theatre in the 17th century and now houses the 19th-century **Teatro della Fortuna**.

The tower was rebuilt after being destroyed in the Second World War. In the centre of the piazza is a 16th-century fountain, the **Fontana della Fortuna**.

Museo Archeologico e Pinacoteca

ⓘ *Palazzo Malatestiano. Tue, Thu and Sat 0930-1230, 1500-1800, Wed and Fri 0830-1330, Sun 1000-1300, 1600-1900, €3.50.*

Fano's town museum and art gallery, entered through a Renaissance arch off the main piazza, has an *Annunciation* by Guido Reni and works by Giovanni Santi and Guercino. Archaeological remains among its collection include a Roman mosaic of a man riding a leopard. Summer concerts are held outside in the handsome courtyard.

The ornately sculpted 14th- and 15th-century tombs of members of the Malatesta family, who once lived here, can be seen in the ex-**Church of San Francesco**, a block to the east.

Cattedrale dell'Assunta

ⓘ *Piazza Clemente VIII.*

Rebuilt in 1124 after a fire, Fano's cathedral has been much changed since, though the Romanesque portal survives, and the interior has a remarkable stone pulpit held up by the backs of four lions, one of which is in the process of nibbling off someone's head. The pulpit was put together in the 20th century from various ancient pieces, some of which may predate the church.

Roman Fano

The most impressive Roman monument in Fano is the huge **Arco d'Augusto**, the main gate into the old town, built in AD 9 by Emperor Augustus. The upper part was partially destroyed in a siege in 1463. What may be the remains of the Roman forum are visible under the Church of Sant'Agostino. Remains of a Roman amphitheatre can be visited by guided tour on Tuesday evenings in summer (corso Matteotti, 2130).

For hotel and restaurant price codes and other relevant information, see pages 10-13.

🍽 Where to stay

Urbino *p19, map p21*

€€€ San Domenico, piazza Rinascimento 3, T0722-2626, www.viphotels.it. Once a convent for the church that it abuts, a stay at the smart San Domenico allows you to breakfast in the porticoes of the ex-cloister and sleep in the convent's rooms upstairs, with the modern additions of a/c and minibars. Comfortable, well-sized rooms have shiny wooden floors and a mix of generic modern furniture and early 20th-century pieces. Newer rooms have views across the piazza Rinascimento to the Palazzo Ducale. Private parking and a great central location. The owners have another hotel, the Bonconte, just outside the city walls.

€€ Ca' Andreana, via Ca' Andreana 2, near Gadana, T0722-327845, www.caandreana.it. 15 mins' drive to the northwest of Urbino, Ca' Andreana is a pretty and secluded house set among rolling hills. There's a great swimming pool with views over the surrounding countryside and a good restaurant, also open to non-guests, which uses organic ingredients produced on the farm for dishes such as tagliatelle with saffron, or roast pork with green pepper and porcini mushroom sauce. The 6 rooms are done up in country farmhouse style, with prints and botanical drawings on the walls; there's a friendly dog, an outdoor table tennis table, and guests can rent mountain bikes or cook for themselves on the wood-fired barbecue.

€€ Hotel Raffaello, Vicolino Santa Margherita 38/40, T0722-4896, www. albergoraffaello.com. In an 18th-century building with a friendly welcome and an excess of marble, Hotel Raffaello has some of Urbino's best views – across the rooftops of the town towards the Palazzo Ducale. Make sure you get one of the 5 rooms

with a view, though: those without are comfortable but fairly plain.

€ Ca' Vernaccia, via Panoramica 10, Pallino, T0722-329824, www.locandaurbino.com. About 5 km from the centre of Urbino, Ca' Vernaccia (also signposted, a little confusingly, as La Tartufara) was rebuilt from the ruins of a local farm. There are good views along the ridges of the hills to Urbino, and there's a restaurant specializing in truffles. Rooms and apartments are simple, and some are on the small side, but nicely done out with wooden beams and spotlessly shiny bathrooms. It's good value too – cheaper than all but the simplest hotels in Urbino itself – though there's no pool.

€ San Giovanni, via Barocci 13, T0722-329055. On a winding street near the centre of town, rooms upstairs with views are especially good value. Bathrooms are tiled and immaculately shiny, though the bedrooms themselves can feel dated; if possible, avoid the ground floor rooms, which are on the dark side of dim.

San Leo and Montefeltro *p23*

€€ Locanda San Leone, strada Sant'Antimo 102, T0541-912194, www.locandasanleone.it. Down the hill a few kilometres from San Leo, this peaceful, wizened *agriturismo* is set in a verdant garden through which a stream flows into a lake. Rustic rooms have bare wood, art and colourfully painted walls. There's a restaurant too.

€ Borgo Storico Cisterna, Santa Lucia Cisterna 12, Macerata Feltria, T335-833 5976 (mobile), www.lacisterna.net. This fantastically isolated ancient farm is 1 km from Macerata Feltria, east of Pietrarubbia. Buildings have been added around a 12th-century tower in a careful and very high quality restoration, with skilful stonework. The interiors, too, have had lots of care – the antique furniture is all from Marche, and the original stone drains have been retained in the ground floor rooms – under one of these are grain silos from Roman times. There's a restaurant, also open to non-guests, and work is continuing to restore and extend a farm that was once important enough to warrant fortifications.

€ Il Castello, piazza Dante Alighieri 11/12, T0541-916214, www.hotelristorante castellosanleo.com. Right on the main San Leo piazza, which the best rooms here overlook; those at the back, with views over the valley, are quieter. Go for one of the good-value antiques-filled rooms, which have much more character than the modern ones. Tiled bathrooms are sparkling, and downstairs there's a café, restaurant and bar, with good options for light lunches including *piadine* (flat bread sandwiches).

€ Locanda il Vicariato, Pietrarubbia, T0722-750031, www.ilvicariato.it. In a restored hamlet (see page 25) at the edge of the Parco del Sasso Simone e Simoncello, *il Vicariato* is an *albergo diffuso*, so your room could be in one of several buildings scattered around the place. Rooms, though not large, are good value and have plenty of character, with wooden beams, open stonework and splashes of colour.

Gubbio *p26*

€€ Bosone Palace, via XX Settembre 22, T075-922 0688, www.mencarelligroup.com. Bang in the centre of town, the hotel is an ornate, antique sort of place with good views over the town from some rooms. The building is described as Renaissance, though the design is more baroque, with ceiling frescoes and gold-trimmed swirls in the smartest of the 30 rooms. Standard rooms are less decorative, but all come with satellite TV, a/c and minibars.

€€ Locanda del Gallo, Località Santa Cristina, T075-922 9912, www.locandadel gallo.it. 23 km southwest of Gubbio on SS298 to Perugia: turn right at Mengara, signposted to Santa Cristina. A 12th-century country house on the ridge of a hill, Locanda del Gallo has a pool and 10 rooms, with some oriental touches in its furnishings. Immersed in green, rural surroundings, it's a peaceful place, good for walks in the hills.

€€ Relais Ducale, via Galeotti 19, T075-922 0157, www.mencarelligroup.com. In 3 buildings near the top of town, the Relais Ducale is a smart, American-Italian family-run place with 30 antiques-filled rooms. Some good contemporary touches, such as modern prints, balance out the occasionally old-fashioned feel of the place. Other big pros include fantastic gardens filled with wisteria and fruit-trees, great views, and – best of all – a secret passage dug for the Dukes of Montefeltro through the shale into the hillside. Suites and junior suites (**€€€**) come with added extras such as massage chairs, jacuzzis and geranium-fringed private balconies overlooking the town.

€ La Ginestra, Valmarcola, Santa Cristina, T075-920088, www.agriturismolaginestra. com. 23 km from Gubbio on SS298 to Perugia, turn right at Mengara, signposted for Santa Cristina. An isolated 30-ha organic farm along nearly 4 km of dirt road between Gubbio and Perugia. 6 separate apartments in 3 buildings include a converted tower, and there is table tennis, a gym, a hot tub, a library and a good pool.

€ Residenza di via Piccardi, via Piccardi 12, T075-927 6108, www.residenzadiviapiccardi.it. On a quiet street in the centre of town, the residence offers simple but spotlessly clean rooms and a nice garden for breakfast. For a slightly higher price, apartments with small kitchens are also available. Bathrooms are tiled and pristine and, although the fabrics may clash, the friendly reception makes this even better value for money.

Pesaro *p30*

There are no hotels in Pesaro's *centro storico*.
€€€ Hotel Vittoria, piazzale della Libertà 2, T0721-34344, www.viphotels.it. One of a small group of hotels in Urbino and Pesaro, **Vittoria**, in an ex-casino, is smaller and more

personal than its big brother the **Savoy**, nearby. It's faultlessly formal: padded leather and polished wood abounds and there are bellboys, fully kitted-out maids and sea views. Rooms are comfortably old fashioned; bathrooms are more modern.

€€ Villa Cattani Stuart, via Trebbiantico 67, T0721-55782, www.villacattani.it. Go for one of the rooms in the 17th-century villa, rather than the rather soulless 'business' rooms in the modern wing of this hotel about 10 mins' drive south of Pesaro. A spectacular swimming pool and formal gardens are the highlights. The business orientation means that rooms come equipped with all mod cons including Wi-Fi and highly professional service.

€€ Villa Serena, strada di San Nicola 3, T0721-55211, www.villa-serena.it. In a house built as an Italian aristocratic summer retreat, guests are looked after by the current Count Pinto and his family. The hotel and restaurant, 10 mins' drive south of Pesaro, are elegant but unstuffy, and there are well-tended gardens and a swimming pool. All of the generous 9 rooms are different, with old furniture and abundant character. Huge fireplaces, a banqueting room and an interesting art collection add to the enormous charm of the place.

€ Badia, strada della Torraccia 20, T0721-405730, www.badiagriturismo.it. A horse-breeding farm inland from Pesaro, Badia does bed and breakfast with 8 simple, smart, new rooms. Guests can sometimes help out in the stables or around the farm with the organic crops.

€ Hotel des Bains, viale Trieste 221, T0721-34957, www.innitalia.com. One of the few hotels near the seafront that doesn't look like a concrete tower block. And while it's not quite stylish, it does retain occasional touches from its heyday in the early 20th century. Rooms are generous and comfortable, with minibars, TV, large gilt-framed mirrors and dated wooden furniture.

Fano *p32*

€€€ Relais Villa Giulia, via di Villa Giulia 40, Località San Biagio, T0721-823159, www.relaisvillagiulia.com. If you can afford it, this is by far the best choice in and around Fano. Set among peaceful vines and olive trees to the north of town, sun streams through old windows into a building originally constructed for the nephew of Napoleon. Nowadays it is an elegant, antique country pile, complete with labrador, swimming pool, lots of books and magazines and old wooden toys. There's a restaurant too, just for guests.

€ Astoria, viale Cairoli 86, T0721-800077, www.hotelastoriafano.it. The pick of the rather ugly seafront hotels, **Astoria** is well placed at the edge of the sandy Spiaggia Lido. The common spaces are unexpectedly contemporary, with wicker furniture and black and white photos, though the rooms are rather dated.

€ Casa Masetti, via Montevecchio 104, T328-230 5099, www.bbcasamasetti.it. Fano's only accommodation in the old centre is this lemon yellow, 18th-century townhouse one block away from the piazza. There are just 3 simple, comfortable rooms, all with private bathrooms, and a shared reading room.

🍴 Restaurants

Urbino *p19, map p21*
There is a good range of eateries in Urbino, from cheap pizzerias catering to poor students to expensive restaurants. Look out for *cresce sfogliate* – an unleavened bread typical of the town.

€€€ Vecchia Urbino, via dei Vasari 3/5, T0722-4447, www.vecchiaurbino.it. Wed-Sun 1100-1600, 1900-0100. A smart place on a quiet side street just inside the city walls, **Vecchia Urbino** has an oil sommelier and a front door plastered in stickers advertising its inclusion in Italian foodie guides. There's an interesting tasting menu, including dishes such as ricotta with honey, a vegetarian menu and some unusual pasta choices, such as *garganelli* with orange and julienne of prosciutto. The meat options are more standard.

€€ Al Girarrosto, piazza San Francesco 3, T0722-4445. Daily 1230-1445, 2000-2300, closed Mon in winter. The prime attraction of this place is its position (and outdoor tables in summer) on the elegant piazza behind San Francesco. The traditional Urbino unleavened bread, *cresce sfogliate*, can be tried as a starter and there are some good risotto options for a minimum of 2 people. After that, grilled meat is the mainstay of the menu.

€€ L'Angolo Divino, via Sant'Andrea 14, T0722-327559, www.angolodivino.com. Tue-Sat 1200-1430, 1915-2230, Sun 1200-1430. Enter by the kitchen and then go downstairs to reach this brick-walled cellar restaurant below street level. The heavily marketed specialities of the house are *pasta nel sacco* – pasta parcels with porcini mushrooms and truffles – and *salami matto* – rather unexciting meat slices in a cheese sauce. There are some other, better, pasta options though, and the meaty 2nd courses (such as rabbit, or lamb with wild sage) are good too. Service can be slow.

€€ La Ballestra, via Valerio 16, T0722-2942. Wed-Mon 1200-1500, 1900-2400. Good food at good prices and a great outdoor seating area under umbrellas on one of Urbino's quiet back streets. There are 42 types of pizza, which also come in 'giant' size, but also plenty of meaty second courses such as lamb or roast pork. Inside there are wooden floors and big lampshades, but most people choose to sit outside if they can. The only downside might be the sometimes eccentrically uninterested service.

€€ Le Tre Piante, via Voltaccia della Vecchia 1, T0722-4863. Tue-Sun 1200-1500, 1900-2330. At the edge of town, with a pretty little wooden patio outside overlooking the nearby hills, this is a friendly spot with good portions of excellent Urbino home cooking, served without pretension. There's a pizza menu

too, alongside tasty choices such as spaghetti with crab and mushroom and steak with parmesan and peppercorns.

€€ Trattoria del Leone, via Cesare Battisti 5, T0722-329894, www.latrattoriadelleone. it. Daily 1830-2330, also Sat-Sun 1230-1430. There are some good vegetarian choices among the more traditional menu options in this little restaurant in 15th-century rooms underneath the Church of San Francesco. There's also a tasting menu of various small dishes that includes **La Cotta** beer, made nearby in the hills of the Montefeltro. Original collograph prints line the walls, though they sit a little strangely with an ugly water feature. It's popular, so book ahead at busy times of year.

€ Al Cantuccio, via Budassi 62, T0722-2521. Wed-Mon 1200-1500, 1900-2330. Friendly and informal, **Cantuccio** is popular with local Italians for its succulent, wood-fired pizzas, also served at lunchtime. There's no outdoor seating, and, when it's full, not much space inside either, but that's all part of the charm. There is a traditional Italian menu, but the pizzas are the thing to come for.

Cafés and bars

Caffè del Sole, via Mazzini 34, T0722-2619. Daily 0700-0200. Down the hill from piazza della Repubblica, this is a multifunctional place, almost always open, either as a bar, café or both. There are several German, British and Irish beers on tap, and light meals, including sausage with roast potatoes, are available. Tables on the street make a great spot to sit and watch Urbino's comings and goings.

I Dolci di Battista, via Raffaello Sanzio 19, T0722-4409. On the corner of the main piazza, is a popular but rather industrial *gelateria*. However, you'd do much better to come up the hill to this place, where everything, including the pastries and the ice cream, is home-made. There are some tables out on the square opposite, and your evening *aperitivo* comes with bar snacks.

Gola del Furlo p23

€€€ Antico Furlo, via Furlo 60, Furlo, T0721-700096, www.anticofurlo.it. Daily 1200-1430, 1930 till late. 23 km southeast of Urbino, at the end of the Furlo Gorge. Mussolini stayed in room 3 of the hotel attached to this restaurant, perhaps to get the best view of his profile on the mountain above. The food here is simple but expertly prepared and presented with an aesthete's eye. Dishes such as poached egg with white truffle, and pasta with pecorino and pepper are elevated above their usual level, and a €25 3-course *menu del giorno* is good value. There's an elegant interior with an open wood fire in season, or an outdoor terrace across the road. There are also 7 rooms, should you want to stay.

San Leo and Montefeltro p23

€€ Il Vicariato, via Castello 10, Pietrarubbia, T0722-75390. Daily 1200-1500, 1930-2300. Another part of the Pietrarubbia project (see page 25), the **Vicariato** restaurant is a stylish place, with candles, an open fireplace, interesting art on the walls and a tasty menu featuring local ingredients such as Montefeltro wines and cheeses, as well as wild boar, lamb and rabbit. Try the excellent cherry wine.

€ La Cotta, via Vecellio, Località Cà Corsuccio, Mercatale di Sassocorvado,T334-252 0471 (mobile), www.lacotta.it. 12 km east of Pietrarubbia. Mon-Wed and Fri-Sat 1900-2330. Transformed from a tumbledown farmhouse into a swish microbrewery complete with a restaurant, **La Cotta** is a popular destination up a steep road from the valley floor. A new wood-fired pizza oven will provide accompaniments to three types of artisan, organic beer: *chiara* (clear – a light ale), *ambrata* (amber – a cool, malty beer) and *rossa* (dark ale – a smooth, warm-toned bitter).

€ Osteria la Corte di Berengario II, via Michele Rosa 74, San Leo, T0541-916145, www.osterialacorte.it. Wed-Mon 1215-2400 (Jul and Aug open every day). This cosy little place just off the main piazza has a good local menu featuring dishes such as pasta with chickpeas, and rabbit with wild fennel. Next door there's a *gelateria*, and beyond that a *liquorificio*, selling all sorts of home-made concoctions, so you don't need to go far to make a real night of it.

Gubbio p26

€€€ La Fornace di Mastro Giorgio, via Mastro Giorgio 2, T075-922 1836. Wed-Mon 1200-1430, 1930-2230. On steps leading down from via XX Settembre, this quality restaurant is in the 14th-century factory of ceramicist Giorgio Andreoli. Despite its aspirations, it's a friendly, unstuffy place. The food is Umbrian with a touch of high-end imagination; expect meats such as pigeon, veal and venison, expertly seasoned with herbs and spices.

€€€ Taverna del Lupo, via Ansidei 21, T075-927 4368, www.mencarelligroup.com. Tue-Sun 1215-1500, 1900-2400. Gubbio's smartest eatery is named after St Francis's wolf, which apparently used to come to this spot for food. It's a formal and expensive place, with thick tablecloths and dark wood furniture, and service can be slow, but they serve good traditional truffle-based dishes.

€€ Locanda del Cantiniere, via Dante 30, T075-927 5999. Wed-Sun 1200-1430, 1900-2230. A cosy place with good pasta dishes and a rare vegetarian set menu (€15, including water and wine). Carnivores are also well catered for, with dishes such as sausage and *rapini* and Chianina beef with truffles. Open brickwork and neutral tones add to the relaxed atmosphere.

€ Ristorante dei Consoli, via dei Consoli 59, T075-927 3335. Sun-Fri 1200-1500, 1900-late. A smart but fairly plain, family-run place on the main street without too many pretensions. There's an €18, 3-course lunch menu, which might feature *umbricelli* with porcini and pork with mushroom sauce followed by *tozzetti* and Vin Santo.

Cafés and bars

Caffè Tre Ceri, Padule, T075-929 1210, www.caffetreceri.it. Daily 0900-1730. Next

to the Palazzo Ducale, this café has tables in the Giardini Pensili overlooking the town.
L'Arte Golosa, via dei Consoli 97. Mon-Sat 1200-2400, Sun 1330-2400. Fight your way through the crowds of locals for Gubbio's best home-made ice cream, from the bargain price of €1.50 for 2 luscious flavours.

Pesaro *p30*

€€ Felici e Contenti, via Cattaneo 37, T0721-32060, www.felicicontenti.com. Wed-Mon 1200-1415, 1900-2300, pizzas till 2330. Pizzas and traditional Marche dishes in a comfortable setting in 2 rooms just off piazza Esedra, deep in the *centro storico*. The walls are adorned with contemporary black and white photographs and there are also seats outside in the piazza.

€€ Osteria di Pinocchio, piazza Antaldi 12, T0721-34771. Mon-Sat 1230-1500, 1930-2400, Sun 1930-2330. An appropriately long room, with sponged blue ceilings, and Pinocchio puppets and dolls decorating the yellow walls alongside past and present family photos. Simple dishes such as pasta with beans are popular with locals, who also come for the excellent home-made desserts. Home-made pasta and large tasty salads make it a good spot for lunch.

€ C'Era Una Volta, via Cattaneo 26/28, T0721-30911, www.ceraunavolta-ps.com. Tue-Sun 1200-1430, 1900-2430. Pesaro's best pizzas are served in the heart of the old centre, in a slightly bizarre restaurant, where wooden tennis racquets, palmistry posters and a fake shed roof decorate the place, and staff wear t-shirts bearing the enigmatic slogan, "Danger – don't drink water...but don't drink life." The pizzas, however, are exquisite – huge, crispy, chewy things that are simultaneously substantial yet melt in your mouth – and it buzzes with people from early until late.

€ La Guercia, via Baviera 33, T0721-33463, www.osterialaguercia.it. Mon-Sat 1200-1600, 1745-2230. Ask to see the large Roman mosaic discovered under the floor of the cellar in this intimate little trattoria

hidden away under an arch, just off piazza del Popolo. The mid-20th-century murals of barrels and rural scenes are much more modern, though also more scratched. Unusually for restaurants in this seaside town, the menu concentrates on the fare of the land: beans and pasta, mozzarella and rocket. Locals fill the benches and wooden chairs, creating a good atmosphere. Home-made desserts are on display under the hanging bunches of plastic grapes.

€ Pizzeria La Boa, viale Trieste 295, T0721-31993. Daily 1100 onwards. A bar, café and pizzeria, **Boa** is a convenient spot for a quick bite between games of volleyball on the beach. Good pizza is available by the slice, or you can get a giant one to take away. Inside and out there is plenty of smart modern furniture to sit at and watch the world go by.

Cafés and bars

360 Creative Cafe, palazzo Gradari, via Rossini 24, T0721-370868. Mon-Sat 0700-2300, though hours may vary. Pesaro's best setting for a tipple or a bite to eat: light meals and good wine are served in the beautiful arched courtyard of Palazzo Gradari. Look out for special events.

Caffè Ducale, piazza del Popolo 21, T0721-34279. Red and black tables and chairs outside on Pesaro's central piazza give this place a decadent air. A good place for an *aperitivo*, with a generous buffet of snacks from 1900, and great people-watching, especially as dusk falls on the piazza, though it tends to clear out soon after.

Gelateria Gianfranco, piazza le Lazzarini 10, T0721-64179. Tue-Sun 1300-2200. Pesaro's best ice creams and a great wide choice of flavours. Try one of several varieties of chocolate, pine nut, or *zuppa inglese* (trifle) flavour containing real pieces of cake.

Around Pesaro *p31*

€€ Osteria della Luna, via Umberto I 6, Gradara, T0541-969838, www.osteria dellaluna.com. Tue-Sun 1030-1530, 1830-2330. One of several decent eateries in the medieval walled town of Gradara, greenery-covered Luna has tables outside and serves good home-made *piadine* as well as pasta dishes such as *caramelle* pasta filled with ricotta, walnuts and porcini mushrooms. Other places to try in the town are the popular **La Botte**, just inside the gate, and **Il Bacio**, on via Roma, with good views up the hill to the castle.

Fano *p32*

€€ Da Maria, via IV Novembre 86, T0721-808962. Tue-Sun 1200-around 2300, but closed when sea is too rough to fish. A popular little trattoria, with a rather wonderful homely old-fashioned style, serving fresh fish. Traditional dishes vary depending on what has been caught.

€€ Osteria al 26, 26 via Giorgio, T0721-820677. Wed-Mon 1930-2330. A hip place with a handful of tables outside in the small, quiet street, where little candle lamps swing from the walls. In the barrel-vaulted interior, big modern art decorates the walls and the cuisine has fusion touches – try the carpaccio or the vegetarian ravioli with radicchio, walnuts and ricotta.

€ Il Cantinone, via Arco d'Augusto 62, T0721-825922, www.ilcantinone.net. Tue-Sun 1200-1500, 1900-2330, pizzas in evenings only. **Il Cantinone** offers a seafood menu or wood-fired pizzas in the evening, either outside under canvas or in the cosy interior, where there are occasional live Portuguese Fado performances.

€ Trattoria Quinta, viale Adriatico 42, T0721-808043. Mon-Sat 1215-1430, 1915-2200. There is a palpable sense of urgency at the **Quinta**, which always seems busy, even out of season, as waiters rush around serving enormous plates of tagliatelle with *frutti di mare* or gnocchi with prawns and courgette, followed by *calamari fritti*, or a mixed fish grill. There are no frills here, just remarkably good and excellently fresh good value seafood. There are tables outside, under cover or not. A quarter of wine is only €1.20, and don't miss out on local speciality *moretta* – a mix of coffee, aniseed liqueur and lemon peel.

✿ Festivals

Urbino *p19, map p21*
Jul Festival di Musica Antica Lots of baroque and early music.
Aug Festa del Duca A historical celebration and recreation of Duke Federico, involving lots of colourful costumes.
Sep Festa dell'Aquilone Kite festival.

Pesaro *p30*
Aug Rossini Opera Festival, T0721-38001, www.rossinioperafestival.it.

✹ Entertainment

Pesaro *p30*
Centro Arti Visive Pescheria, Corso XI Settembre 184, T0721-387651. Look out for exhibitions and shows at Pesaro's contemporary visual arts centre in the spectacular ex-fish market.
Cinema-teatro Sperimentale, via Rossini, T0721-387543. Plays and some interesting cinematic events, such as the **Mostra Internazionale del Nuovo Cinema** (International Exhibition of New Cinema), happen in this 500-seater theatre in the centre of town.
Teatro Rossini, piazza Lazzarini, T0721-387620. Built in 1637, Pesaro's grand theatre changed its name to Rossini in 1855 and now hosts operas during the annual Rossini opera festival in Aug.

◎ Shopping

Urbino *p19, map p21*
As a university town, Urbino has several good bookshops as well as some good fashion boutiques, some selling designer label clothes at knockdown prices.
Raffaello Degusteria, via Donato Bramante 6/8/10, T0722-329546, www.raffaello degusteria.it. Mon-Sat 0900-1300, 1600-

2000. An upmarket deli, **Raffaello** sells wine and organic meat and cheese but also posh biscuits, high quality cookware, jars of all sorts of delicacies and 3 types of the local **La Cotta** beer.

Gubbio *p26*
Mastri Librai Eugubini, via della Repubblica 18, T075-927 7425. Apr-Dec daily 0900-1730. A great selection of handmade leather-bound notebooks and albums, as well as some elegant pens and inkwells.
Tipici Prodotti, via dei Consoli 99, T075-922 0888. Daily 0930-1300, 1530-1900. One of several shops in Gubbio selling a profusion of salami, cheese and pasta. They will happily make up sandwiches on request. Look for the 2 wild boars' heads outside.

Pesaro *p30*
Pesaro has good shopping, with a number of designer fashion outlet shops, lots of smart home and kitchenware shops and a good few delicatessens where you can put together picnics for the beach.
Brendhouse, via Rossini 60, T0721-639121. Tue-Sun 0900-1300, 1600-2000, Mon 1600-2000. One of Pesaro's best designer home shops, **Brendhouse** does a good line in candles and candlesticks, storage boxes and crockery, as well as selling fresh flowers.

☼ What to do

Urbino *p19, map p21*
Yoga retreats
The Estate and Spa, near Urbino, www. thefuckitlife.com. Set on a 160-ha estate complete with a river, 3 lakes, walking trails and its own vineyard, this retreat encourages

you to leave all your worries behind and nurture yourself through yoga and relaxation. Luxury guest accommodation is in traditional renovated farmhouses while the converted barn houses the indoor pool and spa. Massage treatments include reflexology, aromatherapy and shiatsu, while beauty treatments such as facials, manicures and pedicures are also available. After a leisurely breakfast, yoga sessions run 0930-1300, leaving plenty of time for relaxation or visiting local sights. Cookery classes are also available, Week-long courses are full board and should be booked in advance.

⊖ Transport

See also Transport in the Marche, page 8.

① Directory

Urbino *p19, map p21*
Hospital Viale Comandino 70, T0722-301272. **Pharmacy** Farmacia la Medica, piazza della Repubblica, T0722-329829.

Gubbio *p26*
Hospital Via San Francesco, T075-942 2111. **Pharmacy** Farmacia Comunale, piazza Quaranta Martiri, T07-927 2243.

San Leo and Montefeltro *p23*
Hospital Ospedale Sacra Famiglia, Novafeltria, T0541-919399. **Pharmacy** Farmacia Rurale, piazza Dante Alighieri, T0541-916160.

Pesaro *p30*
Hospital San Salvatore, viale Trieste 391, T0721-3611. **Pharmacy** Piazzale Moro Aldo 1, T0721-33135.

Contents

Footprint features

Central & southern Marche

The busy Adriatic port of Ancona, Marche's biggest city, receives many budget flights and is a popular point of entry to the region. It has a quiet old centre, complete with Roman arch, good museums and some exceptional seafood restaurants.

Just to the south, the Parco del Conero is one of Italy's most attractive stretches of coast, with rare wild beaches and green hills that come right down to the sea. Portonovo is a pleasant little beachside village with some good restaurants and hotels and, just around the coast, cliff-top Sirolo has pastel-painted houses and a great beach at the foot of a steep path. Nearby Loreto is the site of Mary and Joseph's house – flown here by angels, or reconstructed by crusaders, depending on who you believe.

Under the ground there's plenty more to see: Europe's biggest cavern is just the beginning of the huge cave network at Frasassi. In the surrounding regional park there are opportunities to walk through gorges and wooden valleys to ancient abbeys and old hermitages.

Back on the coast, Macerata is a little-visited university town with a fantastic contemporary art museum and some good nightlight, as well as an al fresco summer opera season in its distinctive elongated theatre. The surrounding area is rich in Roman remains, most obviously at Urbisaglia, which has a Roman theatre and an atmospheric amphitheatre.

Ascoli Piceno, a buzzing town with a stunning stage-set piazza sitting between mountains and the sea, is the highlight of the Marche's south. There's good contemporary art as well as a Roman bridge and a handful of medieval towers. The high and often snowy peaks of the Monti Sibillini are just a stone's throw away and provide endless opportunities for outdoor activities from hang-gliding and paragliding, to cross-country skiing, walking or kite flying.

The name 'Ancona' comes from the Dorians, who colonized the place in the fourth century BC and named it 'Ankon', which means 'elbow'. It was an important Roman port; later it was destroyed by the Saracens in AD 839 and heavily attacked in both World Wars. Today it is one of the major departure points for ferries to Croatia, Greece and even Turkey.

The small, quiet old centre has enough to keep you busy for a day or two if you're flying or sailing in or out, though the train station and port areas are markedly less attractive. The cathedral is a distinctive building on top of the hill, while below is the Roman arch of Trajan. The archaeological museum has lots of ancient finds, and there are a couple of picture galleries too. To the east, at the far end of viale della Vittoria, is il Passetto, with a strange-looking lift down to a small beach below. Accommodation is not Ancona's strong point, but there are some fantastic restaurants to make up for that, especially if you like seafood. The town also makes a good base for exploring the Conero Peninsula just to the south, a regional park that includes some of Italy's best Adriatic beaches.

Arriving in Ancona

Getting there For flights and airport information, see page 7. Ancona is on the main Adriatic coast train line and there are also direct trains from Rome via Foligno. The main train station, at piazza Nello e Carlo Rosselli, is in the modern part of town to the south; buses run from here to the port and old town centre.

Getting around Buses are run by **Conerobus** ① *T071-280 2092, www.conerobus.it*. Tickets for local buses cost €1.20 (€1.50 on board) and are valid for one hour. Bus 94 from piazza Cavour does the 20-minute journey to Portonovo nine times a day but not always at the most convenient times - check the timetable before you set out.

Tourist information Tourist information office ① *via Thaon de Revel 4, T071-358991.*

Cattedrale di San Ciriaco and Museo Diocesano

① *Piazzale del Duomo, T071-200391. Cathedral: winter 0800-1200, 1500-1800; summer 0800-1200, 1500-1900. Museum: May-Sep Sat 1000-1200, Sun 1700-1900; Oct-Apr Sat 1000-1200, Sun 1600-1800; free.*

At Ancona's highest point, on the summit of Guasco Hill, the *duomo* combines Romanesque, Gothic and Byzantine elements. It is dedicated to the second-century Judas Cyriacus, patron saint of the city. The church was consecrated in 1128, though the crypt has the remains of an older, sixth-century basilica, with mosaics and frescoes, and there was probably an earlier temple to Venus on the same site. The beautiful five-arched portal, in white and pink stone, dates from around 1228. Inside, the cathedral is built in the form of a Greek cross, with a ribbed dodecagonal dome.

The museum, round to the left as you face the *duomo*, has a collection of 400 paintings, sculptures and ancient manuscripts.

Nearby are the remnants of the 97-m diameter Roman amphitheatre. It once held 7000-8000 spectators.

Museo Archeologico Nazionale delle Marche

① *Palazzo Ferretti, via Gabriele Ferretti 6, T071-202602, www.archeomarche.it. Tue-Sun 0830-1930, €4, concession €2, under 18s and over 65s free.*

Marche's archaeology museum is rich in Roman remains, and would be worth a visit just for the elaborately three-dimensional ceilings of the palace in which the collection is exhibited. Diagrams of excavated tombs show in great detail how and where pottery and other remains were found, though there is little information in English. Some of the most impressive pieces are the beautiful metal garlands in room 22, one of which was found on

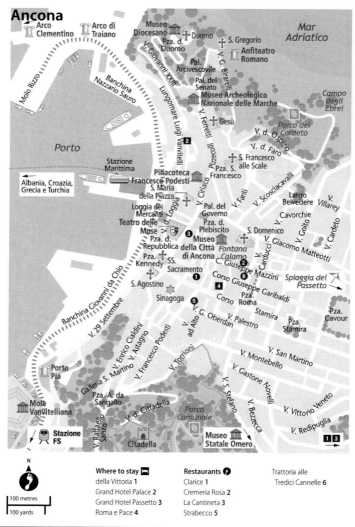

Ancona

Where to stay 🛏
della Vittoria 1
Grand Hotel Palace 2
Grand Hotel Passetto 3
Roma e Pace 4

Restaurants 🍴
Clarice 1
Cremeria Rosa 2
La Cantineta 3
Strabecco 5

Trattoria alle
Tredici Cannelle 6

the skull of an excavated Roman body. Upstairs, an otherwise dull prehistoric section has the skeleton of a bear, which, it is believed, died young due to a bad back.

Pinacoteca Francesco Podesti and Galleria di Arte Moderna
ⓘ *Palazzo Bosdari, via Pizzecolli 17, T071-222 5041, www.comune.ancona.it. Tue-Sat 0900-1900, Sun 1000-1300, 1600-1900; mid-Jun to Sep also Mon 0900-1900, €4.60.*

Seven well-lit rooms make up Ancona's picture gallery. Highlights include Andrea del Sarto's *Madonna with Child and St John,* Sebastiano del Piombo's three-quarter *Portrait of Francesco Arsilli,* and – very much the star of the show – Titian's *Pala Gozzi,* his first dated work, from 1520. It depicts the Madonna and Child with St Francis, St Blaise and Luigi Gozzi, who commissioned the work. Recently restored, the painting is on a raised platform with steps at the back – climb these to see Titian's rough sketches on the back. Look too for the *Pala di San Agostino,* most interesting for its depiction of 16th-century Ancona. Upstairs is the city's rather patchy contemporary art collection.

Chiesa di Santa Maria della Piazza
ⓘ *Piazza Santa Maria.*

A 13th-century church, Santa Maria della Piazza has a beautifully ornate three-part façade, rich in figures and animals, which is being restored at the time of writing. Inside, early Christian mosaics can be seen through glass in the floor.

Piazza del Plebiscito and piazza Roma
A huge statue of Pope Clement XII, from 1738, dominates the city's central piazza. Behind, in the **Chiesa di San Domenico**, is a 1558 Crucifixion by Titian. To the south, the city's second main axis, piazza Roma, has bars, cafés and market stalls; on corso Garibaldi, crossing it, is the beautiful 16th-century **Fontana Calamo**, commonly known as the *tredici cannelle,* or '13 taps', a row of masked heads spouting water into a trough.

Museo della Città di Ancona
ⓘ *Piazza del Plebiscito, T071-222 5037, www.comune.ancona.it. Mid-Jun to Sep Mon 0930-1200, Tue-Fri 1800-2200, Sat-Sun 1000-1300, 1800-2200; Oct to mid-Jun Tue-Wed 1000-1300, Thu-Sun 1000-1300, 1600-1930; free.*

Ancona's well-designed museum gives a good historical context to the city and the region. Most information is in Italian, but there is enough to keep non-Italian speakers interested, including a large wooden model of the city from 1844 and a video and slideshow in the basement.

Arco di Traiano
By the port, Trajan's arch was erected in AD 115 in honour of the Roman emperor who had built the northern quay, increasing the importance of the city. What is left today is only the middle section of what was originally a bigger arch. Pope Clement XII, having further extended the quay, built himself a neighbouring arch in 1738.

Il Campo degli Ebrei
ⓘ *Parco del Cardeto, via del Cardeto, T071-222 4099, www.parcodelcardeto.it. Apr-Sep 0830-2030, Oct-Mar 0800-1730, free.*

At one time the Jewish population of Ancona numbered over 3000, and the restored Jewish cemetery, on a hill above the city centre, is an unexpectedly evocative and moving place.

It was in use from 1428 to 1863, when part of it was requisitioned by the military, and a new cemetery was opened elsewhere. During the restoration 1058 stones were found, and while some have been moved and lined up, others have been left scattered around the grassy area. Around the rest of the park are walks with views out over the sea.

Parco del Conero → *For listings, see pages 59-66.*

① *www.parcodelconero.eu.*
South of Ancona's busy sprawl is a different world altogether: the Parco del Conero, a peaceful, largely rural, protected area, where the hills meet the sea. Portonovo is as bustling as it gets, with a beach backed by cafés and restaurants; to the south, Sirolo is a prettier village, and Numana is a fishing town. There are easy strolls along marked paths through woods to relatively unfrequented beaches, or more serious hikes across the hills. The seafood is excellent, and if you want more in the way of action, it's possible to windsurf or hire bikes or boats.

Portonovo
Less a village than a loose collection of buildings behind the beach and up the hill, Portonovo is the northern centre of the Conero regional park. There are a couple of small shops and the bus from Ancona stops here several times a day (see page 45). Information boards point out walking routes – an easy 90-minute walk goes around the natural saltwater lake of **Lago Grande**. If you walk along the seafront you will eventually come to the **Church of Santa Maria di Portonovo** ① *T071-56307, daily 1700-1900*, in a spectacular and somewhat precipitous position, shored up against the sea.

Sirolo
A beautiful town perched high above the sea in the middle of the Conero park, Sirolo has streets of pastel-painted terraced houses and a path down to a beautiful beach of fine shells and pebbles. Sheltered by a breakwater, the water is clean and clear and excellent for swimming.

Numana
A fishing village at the southern edge of the park, Numana lacks some of the charm of Portonovo and Sirolo, but it does have an archaeological museum, **Numana Antiquarium Statale** ① *daily 0830-1930, €2*, with fascinating exhibits taken from the many Picene tombs discovered in the area. Most impressive are the finds from the tomb of the so-called 'Queen of Numana', actually found near Sirolo, with a chariot and two horses. The metal wheel rims of the chariot are arranged in a case in their original positions, alongside some fabulously ornate pottery as old as the seventh century BC.

Loreto → *For listings, see pages 59-66.*

South of Conero, nearby Loreto is the second most popular pilgrimage site in Europe, after Lourdes. The town centres (indeed grew up) around the extravagant **Basilica della Santa Casa** ① *Apr-Sep 0630-1230, 1430-2000, Oct-Mar 0645-1230, 1430-1900, free*, which, in turn, is built around the simple house of Mary and Joseph, brought from Nazareth in the 1290s on the wings of angels, or by crusaders, depending on which version of the story you read. Inside the Santa Casa, the statue of the black Loreto Virgin is a 1922 copy of the original, which was destroyed in a fire. The **Piazza della Madonna** is an extraordinary, theatrical space and the basilica a grand building, though non-believers may find the wailing and praying uncomfortably hysterical.

Frasassi → *For listings, see pages 59-66.*

Above some of Europe's biggest and most spectacular caves, the Frasassi natural park has tall, steep wooded hills, sharply cut through by the Frasassi and Gola gorges. The attractive hill village of **Genga** is the centre of this isolated, rural Apennine region, but it is so sleepy as to render it more or less comatose for most of the year. The caves themselves are a popular tourist attraction, but in most of the rest of the park you'll meet few people, and even fewer visitors.

Arriving in Frasassi

There is a train station, Genga–San Vittore Terme (8 km from Genga itself), around 50 minutes by train from Ancona. The ticket office for the Frasassi caves is opposite the train station. The caves are well signposted and easily reached by car, off the SS76.

Grotte di Frasassi

ⓘ *Genga, T0732-90090, www.frasassi.com. Guided tours in English Jun-Sep daily at 1115, 1245, 1445, 1615, other times possible if booked in advance; closed 10-30 Jan, €15.50, concession €13.50, 6-14s €12, under 6s free, price includes museum admission. The ticket office for the caves is next to the car park and Genga–San Vittore Terme train station: from here a bus shuttles visitors to the entrance or it's a pleasant 20-min walk via the Abbazia di San Vittore. Speleological visits must be booked at least a week in advance (blue trail 2 hrs 30 mins, €35, red trail 4 hrs, €45).*

Some of the world's most spectacular caves, the Grotte di Frasassi are 1,400,000 years old, though they were discovered by humans only in 1971. A combination of sulphur and water eroded the rock to create the cave system – the paths of the original sulphurous streams are illuminated in blue. The water here, rich in minerals, is quick to create stalagmites and stalactites, which grow at a rate of one or two millimetres a year. So far, 30 km of caves have been explored, and a walkway has been constructed through five caverns – the biggest of these may be the largest single cavern in Europe.

The most spectacular part of the cave complex is the gargantuan **Grotta Grande del Vento**, 200 m high, 165 m long and 110 m wide. The place is so immense, and so bereft of context that one's eyes play tricks. Only when it is pointed out that a stalagmite on the wall is 3 m tall and further away than the length of a football pitch do the massive dimensions begin to sink in. It was here that the cave network was discovered: the moment when someone dropped a stone over the edge into the darkness and heard it eventually hit rock over 150 m below must have been every speleologist's dream.

From here the walkway rises and falls between 20-m stalagmites, and below a stalactite hanging way above that is 7 m long and estimated to weigh six to seven tonnes, before opening out into wider spaces, richly furnished with extraordinary white filigree – it's like being in an enormous melting wax cathedral.

There are more intimate treasures here too – small pools of water sparkling with jewel-like crystals and curtains, and 'organ pipes' of minerals formed by millions of years of drips. There is even a species of blind lizard that lives in the caves, though you'll be lucky to see one. As you go through the caves, you will have various features pointed out – both geological and fantastical. One of the giant stalagmites supposedly looks like Dante. Easier to discern among the weird and wonderful mineral shapes are the camels and the shepherd, as well as a rather sad polar bear. These characterizations had a practical use for the cavers who discovered the network, orientating them in relation to landmarks in the dark.

The temperature in the caves is a constant 14°C. A guided tour – a round trip of about 1.5 km into the mountain – takes about an hour. From the caves back to the car park it's possible to walk alongside a stream for about 1.5 km.

More serious 'adventure' tours, of two levels, are available if you book in advance. Equipment is provided, and the two trails leave the tourist paths and pass through narrow passages to reach two more caverns.

L'Abbazia di San Vittore and Museo Speleo Paleontologico ed Archeologico

① *San Vittore, T0732-90241. Museum Mon-Sat 1000-1300, 1430-1830, Sun and Aug daily 0830-1930, €4, concession €2, free with cave ticket.*

San Vittore's museum complements a cave visit with the geological background: there's a good 3D model of a mountain cut through the middle and the fossil of a 3.5-m ichthyosaur, a sea predator similar to a large shark.

The museum is attached to the **Abbey of San Vittore**, a beautiful Romanesque building, stocky on the outside, slim and elegant within. Founded in 1007, it reached the height of its power in the 13th century, when it was in charge of more than 40 local churches and castles.

Parco Naturale Regionale Gola della Rossa e di Frasassi

① *www.parcogolarossa.it.*

Good walks in the park include a 6-km trail through the **Scappuccia Valley**, north of Genga, taking in a gorge and a wooded valley. You might even meet a rare spectacled salamander. The park has a summer-only **information office** at the Frasassi caves ticket office and an infrequently open office in Genga. A better bet might be to buy a decent map and print out some of the route information on www.frasassi.com.

Tempietto del Valadier and Santa Maria Infra Saxa

In the Frassasi Gorge, 1.5 km west of the entrance to the caves, two buildings sit in a cave above the stream. The smaller **Santa Maria Infra Saxa** (St Mary in the Rocks), from which Frasassi gets its name, was formerly a hermitage and dates back to the 11th century. Inside is a well-tended shrine; the uneven floor is the surface of the rocks below. The second building, the octagonal **Temple of Valadier**, was built in the early 19th century on the orders of Pope Leo XII, who was born in nearby Genga. It fits remarkably snugly inside the cave, from where there are good views down to the gorge.

Macerata → *For listings, see pages 59-66.*

A university town with a pale brick centre, mostly built between the 15th and 18th centuries and enclosed by 16th-century walls, Macerata has a summer opera festival in its distinctive Sferisterio outdoor theatre and one of the region's best contemporary art museums. The student population makes sure that the bars are lively and the surrounding hills have some interesting Roman remains and ancient towns to explore.

The nearby ruins of the Roman Helvia Ricina were plundered to build the medieval town, which was declared a city in 1320. The university was founded in 1290.

Arriving in Macerata

Getting there and around For trains from Ancona (one hour 10 minutes) or from the south, to Macerata, you'll need to change at Civitanova Marche. The train station is just to the south of the centre. There are frequent buses to nearby Urbisaglia and the Abbazia di Fiastra. The town centre is small and walkable. If you're driving, try to find parking outside the narrow one-way systems in the centre.

Tourist information Tourist information office ① *piazza Mazzini 10, T0733-230735, summer Tue-Sun 1000-1300, 1600-1900, winter 1000-1300, 1500-1800.*

Piazza della Libertà

The town's central piazza has at its corner the **Loggia dei Mercanti**. Built in 1504-1505, and an elegant example of Renaissance architecture, it contrasts with the more solid building style that dominates Macerata. These days you can have a coffee or an *aperitivo* on comfy wicker seats under its arches – a prime spot for watching the world go by.

The **Palazzo dei Priori** along the northern side of the piazza is a rather brutal building. Opposite, it is possible to climb the 64-m **Torre Civica**, adjacent to the **Teatro Rossi** (tours at 1100 and 1600, ask at the information office on piazza Mazzini), for views of the surrounding countryside stretching from the Sibillini Mountains to the sea. The original clock was built in 1570 by the Ranieri brothers, who also made the famous clock of St Mark's in Venice – some of the workings can be seen inside the tower.

Duomo

With more than its fair share of baroque grandiosity, chandeliers and portentousness, construction of Macerata's Duomo, on piazza Strambi, was started in the 15th century; the façade was never finished. At opposite sides of the apse are two interesting versions of the same subject: *The Madonna Enthroned with Saints*. Allegretto Nuzi da Fabriano's 1369 triptych has Mary between saints Julian and Anthony Abbot. In the 16th-century version, attributed to Giovanni de Carolis, Julian makes another appearance, this time with Anthony of Padua, and Mary's 'throne' is this time a cloud, on which she and Jesus perch rather precariously.

Basilica della Madonna della Misericordia

Across the piazza Strambi from the *duomo*, Macerata's basilica, built in 1736, is the smallest in the world (the status of basilica is conferred by the pope). Its overwrought interior, an oval design by Luigi Vanvitelli, is extraordinarily decorated with paintings and plasterwork, and the dim, fake-candle lighting creates an eerie feel.

Museo Palazzo Ricci

① *Via Ricci 1, T0733-261487, www.palazzoricci.it. Jul-Aug daily 1000-1300, 1600-2000; Mar-Jun and Sep-Dec Sat-Sun 1000-1300, 1600-2000; free.*

Macerata's excellent contemporary art museum is the best in the region – an intelligently collected and carefully curated selection of Italian 20th-century art. The collection originally belonged to a bank, and the bank manager clearly had an eye for much more than just investment.

Three floors take you through all the important movements of contemporary Italian art, including Futurism, Surrealism and Abstraction. There is some good sculpture too, but it's the paintings that are really exceptional. Almost everyone is represented, from Severini through De Chirico to Morandi and Scipione, who was born in Macerata in 1904. Expertly and lovingly curated, the paintings are well laid out to give a sense of the progression of themes and styles. There's a beautiful 1932 Crucianelli nude, *Nudo su divano*, staring confidently out of the canvas wearing only her shoes, and Carlo Carrà's *Madre e figlio* demonstrates an exceptional use of colour as well as an interesting twist on more usual depictions of motherhood. There are lush landscapes, acutely perceived portraits, Futurist trains and beautiful still lifes. The ground floor also has interesting temporary summer exhibitions.

Pinacoteca and Museo Civico
ⓘ *Palazzo Buonaccorsi, via Don Minzoni, T0733-256361, www.maceratamusei.it. Tue-Sun 1000-1800.*
Macerata's museum and gallery are in new premises between the *duomo* and piazza della Libertà. Highlights of the town's art collection include paintings by Carlo Crivelli and Sassoferrato. A part of the museum is given over to antique carriages, for which the town is famous.

Sferisterio
ⓘ *www.sferisterio.it. Jun to mid-Aug Mon-Sat 0930-1300, 1630-2000; mid-Aug to May Mon-Sat 1030-1230, 1700-1930; on performance days, 0930-1300, 1630-2100; €2 entry plus €2 optional guided tour, book in advance at Macerata Incoming tourist information office, piazza Mazzini, T0733-234333, www.macerataincoming.it.*
Used for the summer opera festival, as well as other musical events from mid-June to mid-September, Macerata's distinctive theatre was originally built between 1819 and 1829 as a sports stadium. The game of *palla al bracciale*, which required a long wall down one side of the arena, was once the most popular sport in Italy, and its stars were some of the best-paid sportsmen in the world in the 19th century. In its day the Sferisterio held around 8000 people – these days capacity is a mere 2800. Built into the medieval city walls, it has a semi-elliptical shape and excellent acoustics that permit opera to be performed here unamplified, though they do stop the traffic outside.

Around Macerata → *For listings, see pages 59-66.*

To the east, attractive hill towns such as **Montelupo** punctuate the route to the over-developed coast. To the south and west, the mountains of the Sibillini begin to dominate. The road to **Sarnano**, itself a handsome town with a particularly striking central piazza at the top of a low hill, is an especially good one. The detour to **San Ginesio** is worth it for the wide-angle panoramic views alone.

Abbazia di Fiastra
ⓘ *www.abbadiafiastra.net. Jun-Sep 1000-1300, 1500-1900; Apr, May and Oct, Sat and Sun 1000-1300, 1500-1900; Nov-Mar Sat and Sun 1000-1300, 1500-1800; €4.50, concession €3.*
Founded by Cistercian monks in 1142, this abbey south of Macerata has been developed as a visitor attraction, complete with café, pizzeria and car park. There's a nature reserve too, with 100 ha of woodland where you may see roe deer and badgers. Material from the nearby Roman remains at Urbs Salvia was used in the construction of the abbey, and occasional pieces of Roman capitals can be seen. Downstairs, under the 15th-century cloister, is an archaeological museum and some spooky cellars.

Urbs Salvia

① *T0733-506566. Jul to mid-Sep daily 1000-1300, 1500-1900; mid-Sep to Oct and mid-Mar to mid-Jun Sat-Sun 1000-1300, 1500-1800; Nov-Feb Sat-Sun 1000-1300, 1500-1630; €6, concession €5.*
To the south of Abbazia Fiastra, the remains of the Roman town of Urbs Salvia, just outside modern-day Urbisaglia, have benefited from EU investment: a network of paths and a beautiful but rather pointless bridge connect the sites, the most impressive of which is the amphitheatre, just off the SS78.

Previously in Picene territory, Urbs Salvia may have been built around the second century BC; it became a Roman colony under Emperor Augustus. It was completely destroyed by King Alaric, the Visigoth famous for the sack of Rome, in the early fifth century. Dante mentions it as a desolate place.

Ringed with tall oak trees, the remains are evocative, especially with the Sibillini Mountains behind them. When the site is closed, there is little to stop visitors climbing the gate to have a look around.

Ascoli Piceno → *For listings, see pages 59-66.*

At the southern edge of Marche, equidistant between the mountains and the sea, Ascoli Piceno has a stunning piazza and two excellent art galleries.

A regional centre, it is a place that is proud of its ancient Picene history: it was the capital of these pre-Roman people. In the Middle Ages it had around 200 towers, a handful of which survive today, as does a Roman bridge. The town centre is an attractive and lively place, and doesn't close down outside July and August, unlike some of its neighbours. There are many old churches and some good shopping streets, which fill up with locals in the evenings. They celebrate **Mardi Gras** here in a big way, and the **Quintana**, a medieval celebration in July and August, sees jousting and lots of dressing up.

Arriving in Ascoli Piceno
Getting there and around If arriving by train from Ancona (two hours) or other places on the coast, change at San Beneditto del Tronto. Pescara, which also has international flights, is slightly nearer (about 90 minutes). The train station is to the east of the town centre. Several buses a day run from Rome, three hours away; there are one of two an hour from San Benedetto del Tronto, an hour away on the coast. The town centre of Ascoli Piceno itself is small and walkable.

Tourist information Tourist information office ① *Museo dell'Alto Medioevo, Palazzo Comunale, piazza Arringo 7, T0736-298204, daily 0930-1300, 1500-1830.*

Piazza del Popolo
The shadows and reflections of passing figures cast on the shiny stones add to the beauty of Ascoli Piceno's showcase piazza. To see it at its best, come in the evening, when the piazza fills with the people of Ascoli wandering, drinking at cafés and chatting.

At one end, the **Chiesa di San Francesco** has an attached Renaissance portico, the **Loggia dei Mercanti**. Look for the plaque in the wall used to check on the sizes of bricks that were once sold here. The church itself was built, rather slowly, between the 12th and 15th centuries, leaving a Romanesque-Gothic hybrid building. Behind it, in the cloister, is what must be one of Italy's most photogenic fruit and vegetable markets. Off the main cloister you may be able to peer through the gate into another smaller one.

Macerata to Ascoli Piceno

This drive takes in ancient abbeys, a Roman amphitheatre and lots of great views of the Sibillini Mountains.

From Macerata, head southwest on the SP77. If you have plenty of time, you could make a detour along the SS77 to the west to visit **Tolentino**, where the Basilica di San Nicola has a nice cloister and some fine frescoes. Otherwise, push on south for around 20 minutes to reach the Romanesque **Abbazia di Fiastra** (see page 52), an abbey set in a nature reserve with some good walks.

Another 6 km southwest along the same road brings you to Urbisaglia and the Roman remains of **Urbs Salvia**, including an impressive amphitheatre (see page 53). Another 15 minutes further south, branch right off the road towards **San Ginesio**, along a stunning ridge road with views to the north and south. San Ginesio has an unusual church, the **Collegiata della Annunziata**, with a beautiful Gothic façade (being restored at the time of writing). Even more striking is the wide-angle vista from the park at the western end of the town, over the Monti Sibillini and Marche countryside all the way to Monte Conero.

Head back on to the SS78: the road bends south as it skirts the eastern edge of the Sibillini National Park. If you have time, you could branch west into the park here, up the Fiastrone Valley towards Fiastra. Further south, **Sarnano** is a pretty, small town with more views and a spiral of medieval streets leading up to the showpiece **piazza Alta** at the summit of its hill, where the 13th-century **Santa Maria di Piazza** has frescoes and a statue of Jesus whose beard is reputed to grow if it's about to rain. There's a *pinacoteca* too, with a Carlo Crivelli *Madonna*.

From **Amandola** (where there is another *pinacoteca* and a couple of museums), another 15-20 minutes south, a road leads to **Montefortino** (with yet another *pinacoteca*) and then west into the **Gola Infernaccio** – Hell's Gorge. Here you can walk alongside the river Tenna and through the narrow gorge, before climbing through beech woods to the **Eremo di San Leonardo**, a hermitage built in the 20th century by a single monk. Just beyond here is a waterfall.

Return to Montefortino and continue east to rejoin the SS78, driving south along winding roads between wooded hills until it eventually joins the SS4. If you have time, turn right here to find the **Castel di Luco**, near Aquasanta Terme. Otherwise, turn left and follow the road to the beautiful town of **Ascoli Piceno**.

On the west of the piazza, the **Palazzo dei Capitani**, built in the 13th century on top of an ancient Roman structure, had a Renaissance portico and loggia added to its courtyard in the 16th century. Next door is the famous *stile Liberty* **Caffè Meletti** (see page 63). The low porticoed buildings around the edge of the piazza were built in the 16th century.

Piazza Arringo

Ascoli's second piazza, the elongated piazza Arringo, is a more staid place, with fountains, a couple of cafés, the *duomo*, the archaeological museum, and the offices of the *comune*, which also contain the *pinacoteca*, the town's excellent art museum.

Pinacoteca

ⓘ *Piazza Arringo, T0736-248663, www.ascolimusei.it. 16 Mar-30 Sep 1000-1900; 1 Oct-15 Mar Mon-Fri 1000-1700, Sat and Sun 1000-1900; combined ticket for all 3 civic museums €6, concession €4.*

Ascoli's art gallery, now reopened after the earthquake of 2009, is one of the region's best, and its grand setting in the Palazzo del Comune adds to the experience. Carlo Crivelli's triptych of the *Madonna and Child* (contemplating an apple) sees the pair joined by saints Lucy, Anthony Abbot and Sebastian, and there are some other good examples of pre-Renaissance art, including several by Crivelli's follower Pietro Alemanno. The anonymous seven-panel story of the *Life of Mary* from the first half of the 14th century is an expressive work despite its primitive proportionality.

Aristocratic rooms are impressively replete with antique furniture and chandeliers, though the lighting isn't great for viewing the paintings. Titian's large depiction of *St Francis Receiving the Stigmata* is especially badly lit. Other works to look out for include Guido Reni's *Annunciation* of 1628-1629 and Tiberio Titti's grandly costumed unnamed woman, painted at the turn of the 17th century.

Several 16th- and 17th-century works depict Ascoli complete with many of its old towers. Romolo del Gobbo's 1905 bronze statue of a flying Paolo and Francesca (see box, page 32) is gravity-defying; while *Fior di Vita*, Cesare Reduzzi's late 19th-century marble nude, is remarkably passionate for someone made of stone.

Galleria d'Arte Contemporanea

ⓘ *Corso Mazzini 90, T0736-248663, www.ascolimusei.it. 16 Mar-30 Sep 1000-1900; 1 Oct-15 Mar Mon-Fri 1000-1700, Sat and Sun 1000-1900; combined ticket for all 3 civic museums €6, concession €4.*

Ascoli Piceno has a rich history of 20th-century art, and an unusually good contemporary art gallery, in a fine, high-ceilinged space. Rotating temporary exhibitions concentrate on local artists, and the permanent collection also has excellent works, including paintings and sculpture by the likes of Severini, Morandi and Trubbiani. Osvaldo Licini, an artist from Ascoli, is represented by his excellent, incisive and characterful portraits, and the exquisite *Paesaggio con l'Uomo* from 1925. His later, abstract work is also well featured in the collection.

Cattedrale di Sant'Emidio

ⓘ *Piazza Arringo. Daily 0700-1200, 1530-1830, free.*

With an elaborately decorated interior, Ascoli's *duomo* is an over-the-top mix of starry blue ceilings and chandeliers. Carlo Crivelli's 10-panelled polyptych from 1473 in the **Cappella del Sacramento**, to the right of the nave, also has its fair share of gold in its ornate Gothic frame, but the painting itself is the artist's masterpiece, full of woe and compassion, especially in the central panel.

Downstairs, the atmospheric crypt is a forest of pillars, and you can peer through a barred door into the town's 15th-century underground ex-cemetery. Next door to the cathedral, the octagonal **Baptistery** (open rather infrequently and usually only at weekends) was built in the 12th century on the site of a previous chapel.

Museo Archeologico

ⓘ *Piazza Arringo, T0736-253562. Tue-Sat 0830-1900, €2.*

The wealth of ancient finds in the area are collected here, and among the usual fragments of engraved Roman stones are some interesting pieces and a couple of impressive mosaics, notably a large and ornate design featuring an optical illusion – the central head can be seen as two different faces, depending on which way up it is viewed.

Chiesa dei Santi Vincenzo e Anastasio
Built in the 11th century, the Romanesque church of St Vincent and St Anastasius, on piazza Ventido Basso, has an interesting façade with 64 stone frames that may once have held paintings. Over the door, the eponymous saints stand either side of the Madonna. In the crypt are some sixth-century frescoes.

Via dei Soderini
At the medieval heart of Ascoli, via dei Soderini has most of the town's surviving towers – they once numbered over 100. One has been turned into a youth hostel. Near here is the **ponte Augusteo**, a Roman bridge across the river Tronto, which has a single span of 21 m and a passageway underneath the road surface, which it is sometimes possible to visit.

Acquasanta Terme → *For listings, see pages 59-66.*

Love of the water here goes back to Roman times, and people still come for the thermal baths, which are rich in minerals. The small town, 16 km southwest of Ascoli, has two Roman bridges: **Ponte di Quintodecimo** and **Ponte Romano**, which were once crossings on the via Salaria. The highlight, however, is a beautiful round medieval castle, **Castel di Luco**, built in the 11th century, which sits on a large lump of rock above the town.

Parco Nazionale dei Monti Sibillini → *For listings, see pages 59-66.*

The region's wildest and most beautiful landscapes are in the Monti Sibillini National Park (www.sibillini.net), spilling across the border between Umbria and Marche. One of the highest parts of the Apennines, it is home to boar, wolves and a bear, and the backdrop to many legends of witchcraft and sorcery. Huge upland plains stretch out beneath its high snowy peaks, carpeted in spring and early summer with wild flowers and farmed at other times for lentils. At the heart of this wilderness, Castelluccio is a remote hill town, often cut off in winter and a great centre for walking and hang-gliding.

The River Nera cuts a narrow valley – the Valnerina – into the hills, a beautifully wooded place winding down from the Sibillini Mountains, with occasional ancient churches along its banks.

Arriving in the Parco Nazionale dei Monti Sibillini
Getting there Castelluccio is almost impossible to reach without a car. There are once-in-a-blue-moon buses from Norcia, but you might never get to leave. If you have no transport, hitching might be an option but best not attempted alone.

Tourist information Before visiting the Sibillini, contact one of the **Case del Parco** ① *in Norcia, for example: piazza San Benedetto, T0743-817090*, to pick up official guides and maps. There is an **information centre** ① *piazza di Castelluccio, Castelluccio, T333-384 2646, Jun to mid-Jul Sat-Sun 0930-1230, 1530-1830, mid-Jul to Aug daily 0930-1230, 1530-1830,* but it's only open in summer.

Castelluccio and the Piano Grande

Despite all the postcards and calendar shots, it's hard to be prepared for the Piano Grande. A gargantuan grassy basin between high mountains, it sprouts a profusion of wild flowers in late spring and early summer. Later, in autumn, as the beech woods turn a thousand shades of orange and rust brown, it is often filled with a sea of morning fog, out of which the hill village of **Castelluccio**, one of Italy's highest inhabited places, pokes into the bright sunshine. In winter it is often bitterly cold, and snow blankets the surrounding hills, some of which have gentle ski runs. Used mostly for grazing sheep and cows, and for growing lentils, it is a serene place, with occasional walkers and hang-gliders punctuating the vast open spaces.

Castelluccio is a tough, frost-bitten sort of place, with little or none of the cuteness found at lower levels. The views are extraordinary, and though there are no obvious sights, the village's situation alone is enough to make it a must-see. In 2008 every street was dug up to lay new cables and pipes, bringing fibre optics to houses that until recently had no electricity – it remains to be seen whether such progress will drag Castelluccio into the 21st century.

All around the Piano Grande there is fantastic walking territory. The Kompass 1:50,000 Sibillini map is one of the easiest to get hold of; the tourist information office in Norcia sells a rather flimsy alternative, or you may be able to find a 1:25,000 CAI map. There are paths, but it's also possible to walk just about anywhere across the unfenced mountains.

For those looking for a longer trek, there are plenty of routes following the Appenine ridge north from Castelluccio, and there's a circuit of the national park known as the **Grande Anello** ('big ring') – a nine-day, 120-km route. Information centres have a good booklet (in English) on the route and there are *rifugi* (refuges) on the way round. For mountain bikers, there's a longer, 160-km route, taking four or five days and also called the Grande Anello.

Lago di Pilato

Just below the ring of the Sibillini's highest peaks, the Lake of Pontius Pilate is said to contain his body. Some stories say that he drowned himself here, others that his body was driven by oxen into the lake. The rare freshwater crayfish that live here, and occasionally turn the water red, add to the mythology surrounding the place. At a height of 1940 m, it is hidden between Monte Vettore and Cima del Redentore, but can be reached by walking from the end of the road leading northeast out of Castelluccio (12 km there and back). From the road, head east to the pass of Forca Viola before turning south up the Valle del Lago di Pilato.

Norcia → For listings, see pages 59-66.

High in the hills at the edge of the Monti Sibillini National Park, Norcia, across the border into Umbria, is much more connected to the hills and the wilderness at its doorstep than its Umbrian counterparts down on the plain. Famous for its truffles, its butchers and St Benedict, who was born here in AD 480, it has a strong identity of its own and feels like a solid mountain town, braced against earthquakes and the cold wind.

Despite being surrounded by wooded hills and valleys, the town centre is, unusually, flat. It was probably settled by the Sabines in the fifth century BC; as Nursia, it was an ally of Rome in the second Punic War in 205 BC. The 14th-century walls surrounding the town remain more or less intact, despite several destructive earthquakes.

The surrounding countryside is some of Umbria's wildest, with the hills of the Monti Sibillini National Park coming right down to the eastern edge of the town. To the north, the isolated Valcastoriana runs up the edge of the park, with some good walking possibilities and easy access to some of the region's most spectacular landscapes.

Arriving in Norcia

Getting there and around There are seven buses a day to Norcia from Spoleto, the nearest station. A car is useful, especially for getting out into the hills, though the winding roads can be slippery and dangerous. There is no public transport across the Apennine border to Marche.

There is free parking outside Porta Romana, at the northeast edge of town. Fairly frequent buses run to and from Spoleto (where you can transfer to the train) from outside Porta Ascolana.

Tourist information Tourist information office ① *piazza San Benedetto, T0743-817090, Tue-Fri 0930-1230, Sat-Sun 0930-1230, 1530-1830 (may be closed in winter).*

Piazza San Benedetto

Norcia's central piazza is an impressive if not entirely cohesive ensemble of buildings, consisting of a castle-turned-museum, a beautiful church and the 14th-century town hall. The information office for the Monti Sibillini National Park is also here. In the centre stands an 1880 statue of the town's most famous son, St Benedict, founder of the Benedictine order and patron saint of Europe. The **Palazzo Comunale** has a portico that was added in 1492 and an attached chapel reached up steps from the piazza.

Basilica di San Benedetto

① *Piazza San Benedetto, T0743-817090, daily 0900-1800, free.*
On the corner of the piazza, to the right of the Palazzo Comunale, the church that marks the birthplace of the first Western monk and the first nun, Benedict and his twin sister Scholastica, is a strangely downbeat place. The Gothic façade has an attractive rose window and statues of Benedict and Scholastica, but the interior has largely been rebuilt and has a disappointingly forgotten air. Downstairs it is more interesting, with a semi-excavated Roman house and some *opus reticulatum* Roman walls built into the crypt, which also has an ancient fresco.

Castellina and Museo Civico

① *Piazza San Benedetto, T0743-817030, www.artenorcia.net, Wed-Mon 1000-1300, 1600-1930, €4.*
Built by the papacy in 1554 to quell Norcian unruliness, the Castellina broods over the centre of the town and now holds its museum. There are medieval sculptures in stone and painted wood, and a terracotta *Madonna* by Luca della Robbia. Paintings include a rather feminine 15th-century *Risen Christ* and a Renaissance *Madonna and Child Enthroned* by Francesco Sparapane from 1530.

Duomo

Norcia's 16th-century cathedral, just off the Piazza San Benedetto., is a fairly dull church worth going into for the fresco of Sts Benedict and Scholastica, alongside the Madonna and a redheaded Jesus, in the Cappella della Misericordia.

Several of the town's other churches are worth a peek inside if they're open: **San Giovanni** has a Renaissance altar, and the **Oratorio di Sant'Agostinuccio** has a nice wooden ceiling. The **Tempietto** is a small, square 14th-century shrine with arches opening on to the street, decorated with bas-relief.

Central and southern Marche listings

For hotel and restaurant price codes and other relevant information, see pages 10-13.

😑 Where to stay

Ancona *p45, map p46*

€€ Grand Hotel Palace, Lungomare Vanvitelli, T071-201813, www.hotelancona. it. Next to Ancona's port, the **Grand Hotel Palace** is a stylishly old-fashioned place, with 40 rooms and 8 apartments. The lounge is big, and rooms have slippers, a/c and views over the sea. Bathrooms are fitted with teal tiles and stainless steel, and the breakfast room on the top floor has great views over the port's comings and goings.

€€ Grand Hotel Passetto, via Thaon de Revel 1, T071-31307, www.hotelpassetto.it. Ancona's best hotel is the epitome of early 20th-century Italian resort cool. Art deco design elements such as leopard-skin chairs and big mirrors dot the spacious lounge, alongside plants and fresh flowers. There is art on the corridor walls and rooms have balconies, views and satellite TV. There's a swimming pool, too.

€ Hotel della Vittoria, via Fabio Filzi 2, T071-55764, www.hoteldellavittoria.com. Halfway up viale della Vittoria, the hotel of the same name makes a convenient stopover, with 18 light, modern rooms with tiled bathrooms and wooden floors but not a lot of character. There's a restaurant, closed on Fri, and parking is available.

€ Roma e Pace, via Giacomo Leopardi 1, T071-202007, www.hotelromaepace.it. A grand old place with an antique feel. Rooms are on the small side but have a/c and jacuzzis, as well as writing bureaux. Breakfast is on the paltry side of generous, but the hotel has a certain degree of retro style.

Parco del Conero *p48*

€€ Hotel Emilia, Collina di Portonovo 149a, T071-801117, www.hotelemilia.com. One of the few stylish contemporary hotels around, **Emilia**, a couple of kilometres inland, has a minimalist, almost Bauhaus feel, and an attitude which is much more laid back than the more buttoned-up Fortino down the hill. Black-and-white jazz photos decorate the walls, there's an excellent contemporary art collection, books and pianos. The bar has colourful stools and outside there is a good pool, plenty of grass and great views. Rooms are elegant and predominantly white. A shuttle bus runs down the hill to the beach.

€€ Hotel Fortino Napoleonico, Portonovo, T071-801450, www.hotelfortino. it. A converted Napoleonic fort in prime position on Portonovo beach, **Fortino Napoleonico** is a smart place with plenty of character to go with its luxuries. There's a bar and a restaurant, and the grand piano gets played every night. You can watch the sun set from a terrace overlooking the sea, and a garden has its own beach access. Rooms attempt Napoleonic style, and even the man who cleans out the minibars wears a bow tie.

€€ Locanda Rocco, via Torrione 1, Sirolo, T071-933 0558, www.locandarocco.it. 7 pale rooms, with light, elegant fabrics, contemporary lighting and bare stone walls create a sophisticated, minimalist feel to this classy small hotel on the edge of Sirolo, built right into the walls at the gate going south out of town. Downstairs there's a restaurant specializing in seafood, with a pleasant outdoor terrace.

Macerata *p50*

€€ Le Case, Locale Mozzavinci 16/17, T0733-231897, www.ristorantelecase.it. 15 mins west of Villa Potenza, **Le Case** is a sprawling place in extensive grounds. The hotel has 13 rooms and a suite, all in a country-house antique style. There's a brick-arched restaurant with a vaguely medieval feel and a fêted and cosy *enoteca* with terracotta walls and an open fire, known for its excellent food. Use of the wellness centre, with a large indoor pool, is included in the price.

€ Agriturismo Coroncina, Contrada Fossa 16, Belforte del Chienti, T0733-906227, www. agriturismocoroncina.it. Accommodation on an organic farm, with woods, a stream and a 'beauty farm', complete with hydro-massage and sauna. The vegetarian restaurant has yellow walls and a terrace, and a 10-course tasting menu.

€ Albergo Arena, Vicolo Sferisterio 16, T0733-230931, www.albergoarena.com. Tucked in behind the Sferisterio, the **Arena** has comfortable rooms without much spare space but with all mod cons, including minibar, TV and Wi-Fi. The best rooms have small balconies with flowers, there's some private parking and the breakfast buffet is uncommonly good.

Ascoli Piceno *p53*

€€€ Borgo Storico Seghetti Panichi, via San Pancrazio 1, T0736-812552, www. seghettipanichi.it. In the Tronto Valley, with views to the Sibillini Mountains, the hamlet hotel of **Seghetti Panichi** is owned by bona fide princesses and consists of a villa, a fortress, a cottage and an oratory decorated with frescoes. It's a friendly place, with gardens and sumptuously decorated suites, rich in colour and filled with antiques. Those in the cottage come complete with small kitchens, and there's a restaurant, pool and sauna.

€€ Palazzo Guiderocchi, via Cesare Battisti 3, T0736-244 011, www.palazzo guiderocchi.com. Courteous and smart, **Guiderocchi** is in an old converted townhouse, with an arcaded courtyard and nice touches such as bowls of apples by the lift. Large rooms have botanical art and flat screen TVs; the suite has a mezzanine and a high ceiling with sloping wooden beams.

€€ Villa Cicchi, via Salaria Superiore 137, Abbazia di Rosara, T0736-252272, www. villacicchi.it. 3 km south of Ascoli Piceno. **Villa Cicchi** describes itself as an *'agriturismo de charme'*, and it's a description that fits,

without the usual frilliness. A country villa built in the 1600s, it is part *Country Life* elegance, part rustic farmer's cottage. 4 of the 6 rooms have ornately frescoed ceilings, and the rest of the place is wonderful, with open fires, and old agricultural equipment in the huge cellars. Mass is still held in the little family chapel, *vino cotto* is still made here, and, despite the pool and the Wi-Fi, the whole place has a genuine feel of antique Marche countryside to it.

€ Aurora, Contrada Ciafone 98, Santa Maria in Carro, Offida, T0736-810007, www.viniaurora.it. Half an hour's drive northeast of Ascoli, **Aurora** is an organic vineyard in the hills where you can stay in 1 of 6 well-equipped apartments. There's a 2-night minimum stay.

€ Language and Art B&B, via dei Soderini 16, T347-531 2280, www.languageandart. com. In the heart of the most ancient part of Ascoli, this friendly and unusually stylish B&B has views over the Roman bridge and the medieval towers. Antiques and piles of books fill the 16th-century house and the 'help-yourself' breakfast comes complete with a freshly made cake every day. Rooms are comfortable and homely, with wooden floors, rugs, and lots of art and ceramics.

Parco Nazionale dei Monti Sibillini *p56*

Castelluccio's only 'proper' hotel is the basic **Albergo Sibilla** – the **Locanda de' Senari** is a much better option.

€ La Locanda de' Senari, via della Bufera, T0743-821205, www.agriturismosenari.it. 25 Apr-Oct, and weekends in winter. On the edge of the village, with great views over the Piano Grande, Locanda de' Senari is a cosy *agriturismo* with 5 attractive rooms and a restaurant offering good, traditional meals using home-grown ingredients. The menu changes regularly, but always includes lentils and local meats. Some rooms have 4-poster beds and there are sloping, wooden-beamed ceilings and large showers. Downstairs there's a roaring open fire.

€ **La Vecchia Stalla**, Astorara, T0736-41758, www.benale.net. In a village on the Marche side of Monte Vettore, this is an attractive thick-walled stone mountain B&B with a very warm welcome. Spectacularly perched 1000 m up, there are excellent walks from the front door. There are just 2 double rooms. The family owns an organic farm, which supplies some of the ingredients for the excellent home-cooked food.

Norcia *p57*

€€ **Il Casale degli Amici**, Vocabolo Cappuccini 157, T0743-816811, www. ilcasaledegliamici.it. A lentil-growing farm with beautiful rustic rooms and apartments in a peaceful spot about 3 km east of Norcia. Rooms are very nicely kitted out with solid wood furniture and metal-framed beds, and the welcome is exceptionally warm, as is the underfloor heating. Half board is a good option, as the attached restaurant (see page 64) serves some of Norcia's best food; breakfast is special too, with lots of home-made produce. Larger rooms are worth paying the extra €10 for – well designed, they have fireplaces, seating areas and big wooden beds.

€€ **Palazzo Seneca**, via Cesare Battisti 12, T0743-817434, www.palazzoseneca. com. Norcia's newest and most stylish accommodation, **Palazzo Seneca** is a '*residenza di charme*'. It's an elegant hotel in a 17th-century palace with a jazz bar (concerts are usually held every Sat night), a library, a refined restaurant and a stylish wellness centre in the cellar complete with sauna, marble massage parlour and a chromotherapy bath. Suites have black marble bathrooms, and there are nice touches such as antique phones.

€ **Casale nel Parco**, Vocabolo Fontevena 8, T0743-816481, www.casalenelparco.com. 1 km outside Norcia on the way to Fontevena. Catering for walkers, **Casale nel Parco** has a good swimming pool under the hills and some simply decorated and fairly rustic rooms and apartments, with plenty of space for a family, that open on to a central grassy area.

There's a restaurant with a large fireplace, they offer traditional *prete* – bed warmers – and can organize horse riding trips.

€ **Grotta Azzura**, Corso Sertorio 24, T0743-816513, www.bianconi.com. Should the Palazzo Seneca be full, or too expensive, this nearby hotel, owned by the same family, would be a reasonable fall-back, especially if you can get one of the better, bigger rooms with tented beds. Smaller, more modern rooms upstairs have balconies, but the style feels a little dated.

🍴 Restaurants

Ancona *p45, map p46*

€€€ **Strabacco**, via Oberdan 2/2a, T071-56748, www.strabacco.it. Tue-Sun 1215-1500, 1915-0300. One of Ancona's great restaurants, **Strabacco** has a wine list as thick as a telephone directory and a friendly, jovial atmosphere that can't all be put down to the amount of wine consumed. The food is a draw too – try the sea bass with olives, tomatoes and potatoes; the chocolate tart is also good. You'll get 4 types of home-made bread and, should you find the wine list a little overwhelming, good-natured recommendations. Ageing wooden seating, fairy lights, theatrical nostalgia and an antique dresser all add to the appeal.

€€ **La Cantineta**, via Antonio Gramsci 1/c, T071-201107, www.cantineta.it. Tue-Sun 1200-1440, 1930-2400, Mon 1200-1440. A traditional and down-to-earth place with red-and-white checked tablecloths and a fantastically eclectic selection of paintings on the walls, from Jesus and Modigliani to a naked bather. Glazed tiles, wood cladding and aproned waiters add to the atmosphere and there's fantastic seafood at good prices. Try the squid salad or the spaghetti alle vongole. Popular, loud and atmospheric, it fills up with Italian families, especially on Sun lunchtimes, when the rest of Ancona seems to shut down.

€€ **Trattoria alle Tredici Cannelle**, Corso Mazzini 108, T071-206012. Mon-Sat 1215-

1430, 2000-2230. A long narrow room with wooden beams, yellow and white tablecloths, a bar and ceiling fans, this is a rustic place that specializes in salt cod, though you might also try the prosciutto with figs.

€ Clarice, via Traffico 6, T071-202926. Mon-Fri 1230 onwards and 1945 onwards, Sat 1230 onwards. With fake bricks, young Italians and a wide range of art, most of it sea-related, **Clarice** is a simple trattoria with no pretensions but plenty of charm. The menu includes local specialities (salt cod, squid with peas) as well as Italian classics (ravioli with tomato, basil and mozzarella), and the atmosphere is friendly and informal. The house wine, at a remarkably cheap €1.03 a quarter, is surprisingly drinkable. Large lamps, a ceiling fan, and tables outside in the quiet side street.

Cafés and bars
Cremeria Rosa, Corso Mazzini 61, T071-203408. Great ice creams in the heart of town.

Parco del Conero p48
€€ Capanina, Portonovo, T071-801121. Daily 1230-1430, 2000-2230, bar 0830-2430. Palm shades and deck chairs outside a pale yellow restaurant on the beach. *Tagliatelle nere* and lots of other fish dishes feature on the menu, and they also do proper pizzas.

€€ Clandestino, Baia di Portonovo, T071-801422, www.morenocedroni.it. Easter-20 Sep Thu-Sun *aperitivo* from 1630, 1930-2400, Sat-Sun also 1200-1500; Jul-Aug open daily. A cool, beach-shack vibe in a place that claims to have invented 'Italian *susci*'. International beers and English crisps are on offer alongside some excellent local wines. The tuna carpaccio is delicious, as is the swordfish salad, and don't miss the chocolate mousse, served with salted breadsticks and clementine oil. Lilies, apple-flavoured olive oil, blue painted wood, a bamboo ceiling and groovy laid-back tunes all add to the hip quotient. Staff float around dressed in white linen, warm bread is served in a paper bag, and the cutlery is as long as your arm.

€€ La Lanterna, piazza Vittorio Veneto, Sirolo, T071-933 1382. Tue-Sat 1200-1430, 1900-2230. A stylish *enoteca* in an ancient building in the centre of Sirolo, with food such as *strozzapreti* pasta with clams and cherry tomatoes, cuttlefish salad and tuna steak. The walls are lined with wine bottles and there is a good selection to drink by the glass.

€ Pesci Fuor d'Acqua, Portonovo, T071-213 9019. Tue-Sun 0900-2200, Fri-Sat evenings only in winter. A café-cum-pizzeria with a big wood-burning oven. You can eat in or take your pizza away to munch on the beach; they also do excellent *cornetti* for breakfast.

Frasassi p49
€ Da Maria, Pierosara, T0732-90014, www.ristorantemaria.com. Fri-Wed 1200-1500, 1900-2230. If you have a car, or fancy a 2-km walk up the hill from the caves, **Da Maria** is the best eating option around. Steadfastly Italian and old fashioned, it has bunched net curtains and peach-coloured walls. Traditional central Italian food doesn't get much better than this, and it's immensely popular with locals, who flock here for Sun lunch and keep the place buzzing, as do the home-made grappas and bitters. If you want something nearer to the caves, **La Cantina**, favoured by cave guides, is the best option in San Vittore.

Macerata p50
€€ La Volpe e l'Uva, via Berardi 39, T0733-237879, www.volpeeuva.it. Mon-Sat 1800-0200. A traditional, brick-vaulted *osteria*, on a quiet side street, that sells wine long into the night. Dishes include penne with sausage and pecorino cheese and lots of local veal.

€€ Osteria dei Fiori, via Lauro Rossi 61, T0733-260142, www.osteriadeifiori. it. Mon-Sat 1200-1500, 1900-2300. Run by 3 siblings since 1980, this proponent of slow food offers a friendly atmosphere and home cooking with a sprinkling of invention. Antipasti include walnut bread with oranges, olives and ham, and the pasta, including *vincisgrassi* (the local version of lasagne, with many thin layers of pasta), is excellent. Service is quick and efficient and, though the internal decoration is nothing to write home about, there is also some outdoor seating.

€ **Il Pozzo**, via Costa 5, T0733-232360, www.ilpozzo.com. Wed-Mon 1230-1430, 1800-0300 (kitchen from 2000), daily in summer. Businessmen, ageing locals and hip students all frequent this vaulted bar-cum-pub at lunchtime for its excellent buffet. For €10 you can have as many servings as you like of a selection of local dishes, and a generously sized glass of wine is thrown in too. Not only is it a bargain, it's an excellent way to try Marche cuisine without necessarily knowing what everything's called. In the evenings there's an à la carte menu and the bar keeps it buzzing until the early hours. There is sometimes live music, and photos of past concerts decorate the walls.

Cafés and bars
Faber Café, Vicolo Ferrari 10/12, T0733-262950, www.fabercafe.it. Tue-Sun 1900-0200. In the middle of Macerata, a slick bar that does something different – its Italian owner is a fan of beer, and since 2007 has been trying to educate his fellow Maceratans. There are 5 excellent beers on tap, and plenty more in bottles. Ask for a special beer cocktail or chat about real ale in a setting that feels like the most metropolitan of cocktail bars. English and Scottish beers predominate, but there are also good Italian ales.

Ascoli Piceno *p53*
€€ **Trattoria dell'Arengo**, via Tornasacco 5, T333-471 3333. Tue-Sun. Just off piazza Arringo, this is a popular, good value, traditional place with art on the walls under arches. There are red fairy lights and golden tablecloths, and the menu is dominated by pasta and grilled meat.

€ **Da Middio**, via delle Canterine 53, T0736-250867. Tue-Thu 0830-1630, Fri-Sat 0830-1630, 1830-2400. Bright lights, paper tablecloths and no written menus: Da Middio offers up great local food with little fuss for very little money. A €16 fixed-price menu gets you wine and 3 of 4 courses. Fish features strongly and there are some excellent pasta dishes. Turn up early for a seat, especially in the evening, or be prepared to wait at the bar with some boisterous locals.

Cafés and bars
Caffè Meletti, piazza del Popolo, T0736-259626, www.caffestoricomeletti.it. Daily, early till late. A destination in its own right, Meletti is a Liberty-style café that makes its own *amaro* to a traditional local recipe, featuring aniseed. It's also a fine spot for a coffee, on the town's central piazza, with large gilt-framed mirrors and elegant furniture.
Il Tannino Orgoglioso, piazza Ventidio Basso, T320-698 0070. Daily 1130-1400, 1930-0200. A lively wine bar with a cross-vaulted ceiling, stone walls, wooden tables and loud music. Snacks are available to accompany the wine, which flows late into the night.
Yoghi, piazza Arringo 39, T0736-257414. Mon-Sat 0730-2400, Sun 0830-1400, 1615-2400. Nominally a yoghurt bar, **Yoghi** has a good selection of fruit that you can mix as you wish, but there's also a chocolate theme for the less healthy – the great biscuits, hot chocolate thick enough to stand a spoon up in and bars of handmade chocolate all give this brick-vaulted café on piazza Arringo a decadent feel.

Parco Nazionale dei Monti Sibillini *p56*
In Castelluccio, **La Locanda de' Senari** (see page 60) also has a good restaurant.
€ **Panini allo Scarafischio**, what appears to be little more than a burger van in Castelluccio's piazza-cum-car park is actually one of the best places around to buy fine sausages, cured meats and cheese, any of

which can be made into great panini, hot or cold. Expect conversation about world economic problems and a plastic beaker of wine to go with your ham sandwich.

€ Taverna Castelluccio, via Dietro la Torre 8, T0743-821158, www.taverna castelluccio.it. Homely and simple, with blue and white tablecloths, and pictures on the walls inside and a couple of tables outside on the street, the taverna offers a traditional local menu using almost all local, natural ingredients such as lentils, beans, beef and pecorino cheese.

Norcia p57

€€ Granaro del Monte, via Alfieri 10, T0743-817551. Daily lunch and dinner. Norcia's most popular restaurant, underneath the **Grotta Azzurra** hotel, is a huge place, with cosy rooms inside, near the roaring fire, or tables outside. Meat cooked on the open fire is the speciality but there are plenty of truffle and lentil dishes too.

€€ Il Casale degli Amici, Vocabolo Cappuccini 157, T328-861 2385, www. ilcasaledegliamici.it. 1245-1500, 1945-2130; may be closed during the week in winter – ring ahead to check. Up the hill out of Norcia, **Casale degli Amici** is an *agriturismo* (see page 61) with a fantastic restaurant. The lentils are home grown, the salami is of the highest quality, the pasta is melt-in-your-mouth fresh and the meat is expertly cooked. In a large, barrel-vaulted room with bare stonework and lights suspended from wires, it's also an atmospheric place, and one that is popular with locals. Well worth the trip.

€€ Taverna de' Massari, via Roma 13, T0743-816218, www.tavernademassari.com. Wed-Mon lunch and dinner. This little place just off piazza Santi Forti has checked tablecloths and a 'typical' menu, or you could splash out on a truffle menu. A la carte dishes such as tortellini with cream and truffles, or Castelluccio lentils with grilled sausage, are hearty and typically Norcian.

€ Trattoria del Francese, via Riguardati 16, T0743-816290. Sat-Thu (daily Jul-Sep)

1200-1430 (1500 in summer), 1930-2130. A small place with an open fire on which the meat is cooked, **Trattoria del Francese** makes few concessions to stylishness – the wood cladding is ugly, there are polystyrene tiles on the ceiling, and shields, plates and certificates decorate the walls. The food, however, is excellent, and it fills up with loyal Italians. There's a separate truffle menu and the *contorni* are unusually good.

⊛ Festivals

Ancona p45, map p46
Jul-Aug Ancona Jazz, T071-207 4239, www.anconajazz.com. The main focus for the city's music festival is a fortnight or so at the end of Jul and beginning of Aug, but other events are scattered through the year. Free concerts take place in piazzas, while ticketed events happen in the Teatro delle Muse and other locations around town. Recent artists have included Pat Metheny and Brad Mehldau.

Macerata p50
Jul-Aug Sferisterio Opera Festival, T0733-230735, www.sferisterio.it. The summer opera season is short but sweet. There are usually 3 or 4 performances of 3 different operas, from mid-Jul to mid-Aug, and an enlightened ticket policy means that while front-row seats go for €150, there are unreserved standing tickets for just €15. Also look out for other gigs and events at the **Sferisterio** during summer.

⊙ Shopping

Ancona p45, map p46
The narrow via degli Orefici has some small boutique shops, including **Papier**, selling books and art.

Books
Feltrinelli, Corso Garibaldi 35, T071-207 3943. A good selection of books and one of the few shops in Ancona open on Sun.

Gulliver, Corso Mazzini 27, T071-53215. A decent selection of guidebooks.

Food

Bonità delle Marche, Corso Mazzini 96/98, T071-53985. A delicatessen with lots of choice for putting together a good picnic.

Norcia *p57*

Antica Norcineria, Piazza del Comune 11. Daily 0700-1330, 1600-2000. A decent range of bread, cheese and fruit right in the middle of town. And there's an *enoteca* next door should you want a bottle of Sagrantino.

⏱ What to do

Parco del Conero *p48*
Boat trips

Traghettatori del Conero, T071-933 1795, www.traghettatoridelconero.it. Daily 0930 and 1030 from Numana, €20, concession €10, 1030 from Sirolo, €15/10. Trips around the coast last about 3½ hrs: ring to check timetable.

Cycling

Conerobike, via Peschiera 30/a, Sirolo, T071-933 0066, www.rivieradelconerocycling.it. The organization promotes mountain biking in the Parco del Conero – they have a map of the park that you should be able to get from tourist information offices, and they also rent bikes, by the hour, or from €14 per day.

Watersports

PWB, Portonovo, T333-526 8997. Along the beach from Portonovo, **PWB** rent out windsurfing boards and also offer tuition – a course of 4 lessons costs €150 plus €30 insurance. They have surfboards too, but these get little use as the waves are seldom good enough.

Parco Nazionale dei Monti Sibillini *p56*

The Monti Sibillini National Park is a great setting for year-round activities, from paragliding and hang-gliding, to cross-country skiiing, walking or kite flying.

Cycling

Sibillini Cycling, in Sarnano, on the Marche side of the park, T334-743 8418, or T+44(0)208-133 5441 in the UK, www.sibillinicycling.com. Apr-Oct. Rent mountain bikes from €15 a day and offer free car cycle carriers and helmets. They also offer guided 'bike days' and short touring holidays.

Hang-gliding andparagliding

Prodelta, T339-563 5456, www.prodelta.it. Hang-gliders and paragliders flock from all over Europe to Castelluccio and the **Piano Grande**, where the vast expanses of grassy slopes and a large, smooth landing site make it a perfect spot for flying, especially for beginners.

Throwing yourself off the top of a mountain and gliding down on the thermals must be one of the best ways to see the Sibillini. No experience is necessary, and a tandem flight with an experienced, licenced glider gives you most of the exhilaration, without some of the fear.

Ring in advance to reserve a flight – 1 day's notice may be enough during the week, but you usually need to book at least 3 or 4 days ahead for weekend flights. It may sometimes be necessary to cancel flights because of bad weather.

Horse riding

Centro Ippico Oxer, Paganelli, T339-533 4468, www.escursioniacavallo.it. The **Oxer Riding Centre**, about 7 km from Norcia, offers excursions on horseback in the Sibillini, ranging from a gentle afternoon's walk to longer treks on ancient mountain tracks, camping or staying in refuges or on farms.

Rafting

Gaia, Località Biselli di Norcia, T338-767 8308, www.asgaia.it. On the edge of the Sibillini, near Norcia, there are opportunities for rafting downstream on the Corno River, both slowly and quickly. If a meandering journey is more your thing, the **Biselli Gorge** is a good route, with opportunities to swim.

There are also rapids that can be tackled by those after a little more adrenaline, and places where the brave can dive into streams from a 'natural diving board'. **Rafting Umbria**, T348-351 1798, www.raftingumbria.com.

Skiing

There are ski lifts on **Colle le Cese**, to the south of Castelluccio, as well as at **Monte Prata**, to the north, and you can do cross-country skiing across the plains. It's a stunningly beautiful place to ski, though the slopes are relatively short and not especially steep. The snow can be unreliable, however, even in the middle of winter, and there is little infrastructure except at weekends.

Walking

For a serious trek, the **Grande Anello dei Sibillini** (Great Sibillini Ring) is a 120-km, 9-day route. The park website (www.sibillini. net) also has details (in Italian) of many 1-day walks you can do, or you can grab a decent map (see page 56) and strike out on your own. Especially up high in the mountains it's possible to walk just about anywhere, but make sure you are properly equipped – it's quite possible for the weather to close in.

Monte Guiadone, near Castelluccio

From the belvedere just above Rifugio Perugia, overlooking the Piano Grande to the south of Castelluccio (where there is parking), a good and fairly level 8-km walk winds around the contours of the mountains above the plain, passing through beech

woods before ending either on a grassy spur of the mountain that juts north, or, if you feel like a short ascent, at the 1647-m summit. The views all along this route are stunning.

From the belvedere, follow the little-used road to the right that heads gently downhill toward the wood. Pass by ski lifts on your right before branching left along a path as the road descends to Piano Piccolo, another plain, to the right. Follow this path through small beech woods and along the sides of exceptionally steep grassy slopes high above the Piano Grande.

Alternatively, for a higher route, with views across the Piano Grande to the usually snow-capped Monte Vettore and Cima del Redentore, head northwest from the belvedere around the western edge of the plain below. This route, which can also be done by mountain bike, eventually takes you into Castelluccio.

Directory

Ancona *p45, map p46*
Hospital Ospedale Umberto I, largo Lorenzo Cappelli 1, T071-202095.
Pharmacy Farmacia Centrale, corso Mazzini 1, T071-202746.

Macerata *p50*
Hospital Via Santa Lucia 2, T0733-2571.
Pharmacy Eredi Cappelletti, Corso Matteotti 23, T0733-230871.

Ascoli Piceno *p53*
Hospital Ospedale Generale Provinciale CG Mazzoni, 1 Via degli Iris 1, T0736-3581.
Pharmacy Corso Giuseppe Mazzini 144, T0736-259163.

Contents

Background

History

Umbri, Etruscans and Picenes

Disproving the common belief that Italian culture started with the Romans, Umbria and Marche are rich sources of some sophisticated pre-Roman remains. The first populations probably migrated to central Italy from eastern and central Europe around 1500 BC, initially to the fertile plains around Perugia, then increasingly into the hills.

Earliest inhabitants

Little is known about the Umbri, the first sophisticated, organized civilization in the region. Pliny the Elder, writing in the first century AD, called them the oldest people in Italy, and their lands probably stretched to cover much of modern-day Tuscany and Marche as well as Umbria. There was a distinct and strict Umbrian social structure, probably based on military rank. The Iguvine or Eugubian Tablets, bronze plates discovered by a farmer near Gubbio in the 15th century, are engraved with Umbrian inscriptions that tell of religious rituals including sacrifices.

Etruscan culture

As the Etruscans spread from the northwest, the Umbri were pushed east, so that by around 700 BC the River Tiber was the dividing line between the two cultures, and the Etruscans controlled previously Umbrian towns such as Perugia and Orvieto. They traded extensively with the ancient Greeks, to the extent that around three-quarters of all Ancient Greek pottery discovered to date has been found in Italy.

Etruscan civilization was highly developed, of unknown origins, and with a mysterious non-Indo-European language. Modern genetic experiments on people living in the region suggest their Etruscan ancestors may have come from the Eastern Mediterranean. They seem to have been a loosely affiliated society, without a centralized power base. No history written by the Etruscans exists, though there are plenty of funerary inscriptions. The Etruscan tombs outside the walls of Orvieto are a rich source of information. There are also Etruscan tombs outside Perugia, and many sarcophagi in its archaeological museum. These carved stone coffins often portray the deceased reclining on the lid.

In comparison with ancient Greece, women seem to have been given more prominence in Etruscan society, with tombs possibly suggesting a matriarchal line of descent. Etruscan women, unlike Greek women, attended banquets, and some Etruscan carvings show affection between couples, which is usually absent from Greek depictions.

There is debate about the extent to which the Etruscans influenced the Romans – certainly much of Etruscan architectural style was adapted by the Romans, and some go as far as to suggest that the name Rome itself may be Etruscan. Ancient Etruscan walls and city gates can be seen in Orvieto and Perugia, where Emperor Augustus later added his stamp to one of the Etruscan gates.

The Picenes are the most obscure of the region's ancient peoples. A warlike bunch, they inhabited a small strip of present-day Marche, giving their name to the town of Ascoli Piceno. Many were buried in full battle garb, with swords (imported from the Balkans) and spears.

In 309 BC Perugia was defeated in battle against the Roman army and gradually, over the next 150 years, the entire Etruscan, Umbrian and Picene region fell under the control of Rome.

The Roman Empire

A power struggle followed the murder of Julius Caesar in 44 BC. Caesar's great-nephew Octavian forced Mark Antony's brother Lucius Antonius out of Rome; when he took refuge in Perugia, Octavian (now Emperor Augustus) destroyed the city, and with it the last remnants of Umbrian independence. The *Arco Etrusco* (Etruscan Arch) still bears the inscription that the emperor had placed on it – 'Augusta Perusia' – renaming the city after himself and stamping his authority on the region.

By this time Rome was already the dominant force in the whole region. Historians disagree about the exact level of the Etruscans' influence on the early Roman Empire: some believe that they may have had an important part to play in the founding of Rome itself. Once the two powers were competing for control of the region, however, the loose structure of Etruscan government was no match for the centralized power of Rome.

Roman settlements

The important via Flaminia, which connected Rome with the Adriatic at Fano, had a major influence on the region for many centuries. A part of the road, paved with stones on which Roman cartwheel grooves are still visible, can be seen at Carsulae, where it passes through the *Arco di Traiano* (Trajan's Arch), and much of the original Roman route is still used, including, at the Gola del Furlo, a tunnel through the rock constructed by Vespasian in AD 77.

As trade flowed through the region, Roman towns grew up, and earlier Umbrian towns expanded. Umbria became increasingly prosperous and strategically important. Romans took their holidays in Umbria, and emperors partied at the Fonti del Clitunno. Roman towns such as Interamna Nahars (Terni), Spoletium (Spoleto), Fulginium (Foligno) and Perusia (Perugia) thrived; historians described Narnia (Narni) in such glowing terms that CS Lewis later borrowed its name for his heavenly fictional world.

Roman Carsulae, in the hills north of Narni, grew up almost entirely because of its position on the road, and became a staging post complete with a theatre and amphitheatre complex, temples and a large triumphal arch. The via Flaminia was subsequently re-routed around the town, however, and an earthquake may have hastened its demise. Abandoned for centuries, it is now an important and idyllic archaeological site.

Life was not always simple for the Romans – they suffered one of their worst military defeats here in 217 BC, when the Carthaginian general Hannibal, having led his army, complete with elephants, over the Alps, lured a Roman army under Flaminius into an ambush and killed at least 15,000 soldiers.

Though the region's urban buildings are often of medieval origin, the layouts of many towns still follow the original Roman city plan, with a central piazza where the Roman forum once stood, and a main street that follows the route of the original east-west *decumanus maximus*. Towns such as Assisi were built over Roman foundations, and the front section of the original Roman temple still stands, now adapted into a church.

Almost everywhere you can find Roman carvings and columns reused by subsequent generations – the Tempietto sul Clitunno was thought to be a Roman temple, until it was realized that early Christians had reused parts of earlier Roman ruins to build their church. Many other churches in the region feature recycled Roman capitals and stones.

Eventually, the road that had given the region so much prominence also brought problems. As trade had travelled along the via Flaminia in the years of the Roman Empire, so Vandal and Visigoth invaders used it in subsequent centuries, and with the fall of the Western Empire the region was subjected to many major battles that ushered in a new, less ordered era.

The Dark Ages – early Christian and Gothic

As the Roman Empire declined and fell, into the post-Roman (Byzantine) era stormed the eastern Germanic Goths. Umbrian towns were destroyed as they found themselves caught in a strategically significant position between the two battling forces. With the disintegration of central government the region fragmented; the hills of Umbria, and the monastic traditions and practices they gave birth to, were to be essential to the survival of western Christianity.

The Lombards and the Duchy of Spoleto

The Goths ruled central Italy until the western Germanic Lombards, under King Alboin, successfully invaded in AD 568. The Lombards' Duchy of Spoleto covered most of modern-day Umbria, though the Byzantines retained a strip of central Italy from Rome to the Adriatic, including Narni and Perugia, cutting off the Duchy from the Lombard centre of power to the north but also giving it a degree of independence.

The Lombards had arrived with a fearsome reputation, but as they settled in the region they became less warlike, gave up their Arianism to embrace Catholicism, and contributed to the construction of abbeys. It was, eventually, a time of renewed stability and an era of importance for Spoleto, though little remains from the Lombard era – the Chiesa di San Pietro in Valle is an exception.

To the north, the Lombards overstretched themselves when they invaded Ravenna, upsetting the pope. In AD 754, Pope Stephen III consolidated the papacy's earthly power when he asked the Franks, under Pepin the Short and subsequently his son Charlemagne, to take up arms against the Lombards. Though the Duchy of Spoleto continued to exist as an entity until 1250, the balance of power had swung away from the Lombards, and the eighth century marked the beginning of a long and often uneasy relationship between the Franks and the pope; nominally partners in the Holy Roman Empire they were often bitterly opposed as they fought for economic control, not just of Italy but of the whole of Western Europe.

Birth of monasticism

While these power struggles were being played out, in the Umbrian hills, Benedict and Scholastica were born in Norcia in AD 480; they initiated a long spiritual tradition in the region that looked not to the grandiose papal style of Rome but to a more humble, meditative religion, which centuries later would culminate in the philosophy of St Francis.

At the same time the Benedictine influence gave to Western Europe a quiet – and at the time unheralded – tradition of learning, in the process preserving history and literature. Benedict founded 12 communities of monks and his 'Rule', the code by which the monks lived, was highly influential, though he never set out to found anything as far-reaching as a monastic order and was not canonized by the Roman Catholic Church until 1220. The Rule, actually a book of precepts summed up in the words *pax, ora et labora* ('peace, prayer and work'), was designed to set the foundations for religious communities living together. Widely adopted by monks and nuns ever since, it has been so successful that St Benedict is generally regarded as the founder of Western monasticism, his sister as the first nun.

The pope and the Holy Roman Empire

Struggles between the pope and the state have a long history in Italy, and Umbria and Marche have always been either involved in or affected by them.

In AD 776 the Duchy of Spoleto fell to Charlemagne and his Frankish army. Twenty years earlier, Charlemagne's father Pepin the Short, having captured Ravenna from the Lombards, had given it to the papacy in return for influence and titles. The Duchy of Spoleto was now also given to the pope, though Charlemagne retained the right to name its dukes. In AD 800, Pope Leo III crowned Charlemagne Holy Roman Emperor. It was a hugely significant moment for Western Europe, and central Italy was largely shaped by it for the next 1000 years.

In creating the notion of a Holy Roman Empire, Charlemagne built an entity to rival the power of the Byzantine Church to the east, merging Germanic power with historical memories of the Roman Empire and the spiritual authority of the papacy. At the same time the Papal States were born and the pope became involved in temporal power to an unprecedented extent, becoming a political and economic power as well as a spiritual one.

Guelphs and Ghibellines

The tensions created by this relationship between pope and emperor, and the vexed question of whether the Church gave authority to the emperor or vice versa, were played out at local levels, with powerful families and towns taking (and often switching) sides to suit their own ends.

By the 12th century, the faction on the side of the papacy had become known as the Guelphs; those in favour of the emperor were the Ghibellines. ('Guelf' was probably derived from the Bavarian dukes of the Welf, and 'Ghibelline' from the rival Hohenstaufens of Swabia, who used Waiblingen, the name of their castle, as a battle cry.) Associations were loose, however, and more often local than national. Guelphs often came from rich mercantile backgrounds and Ghibellines from agricultural estates. Born in Assisi in 1181, St Francis himself fought in this strife, taking part in battles against Perugia, where he was captured and imprisoned.

This background of centuries of local squabbles and bitter rivalries helped to create the Umbria and Marche landscape that still exists today, with fiercely protected castles and walled hill towns guarding local *comuni* (communes/municipalities), and strongly held local identities. Castles such as Gradara (see page 31) date from this period, and even important farms had their own watchtowers and defences, some of which still survive.

At times, larger forces washed over these local battles. When Frederick Hohenstaufen, known in Italy as Barbarossa, became emperor in 1152, he marched south, brutally overpowering and often destroying Umbrian cities that stood up to him, such as Spoleto. This imperial violence did not mean, however, that papal governors were received any more favourably – the rich, noble families of Perugia were particularly unhappy to be governed from Rome.

Pope Innocent III came to Umbria in 1216 to try to firm up his authority, but he died, probably poisoned, in Perugia. The regional antipathy towards the pope was political rather than religious, but a new-found religious enthusiasm was inspired by St Francis and had a profound influence on the region. And while it was often an anarchic and bloody period, in some ways the local competition and one-upmanship also paved the way for the architectural and artistic flowering of the Renaissance, as well as fostering the area's independent spirit.

The Renaissance and the end of self-government

The first green shoots of the Renaissance began to appear early in the region, when the papacy was split between Avignon and Rome in the 14th century – the so-called Western Schism. With Europe's attention focused elsewhere, Umbria and Marche were left largely to their own devices, and the *comuni*, which already enjoyed a degree of independence, flourished. Many of the structures of 21st-century Umbria and Marche date from the 14th and 15th centuries, years when the *comuni* had enough power and economic strength to define their own destinies.

Papal domination

It would, however, be wrong to characterize the medieval period as a golden era for the region. Bitter infighting continued, and it was a time notable as much for its bloodiness as for its cultural blossoming. Foreign *condottieri*, or mercenaries, were hired to fight on behalf of local towns and cities, increasing the violence. The streets of Perugia are said to have flowed with the blood of the murdered. Then there was the Black Death, which killed more than half the population in 1348. There was no understanding that bubonic plague was passed on by fleas on rats, and the disease recurred many times after the main outbreak was over. And there were earthquakes too. Eventually, weakened by fighting between themselves, the towns and cities of the region all fell to the papacy, and long centuries of neglect followed.

La Guerra del Sale – the Salt War – is a good example of the different military and economic influences of the times. In 1540, Pope Paul III told the citizens of Perugia that thenceforth they would be forced to purchase only papal salt, at a price that was more than double what they were currently paying. The justification given was that the income was needed to support the papal troops. The people of Perugia were not impressed and, after the failure of negotiations, war broke out between the city and the papacy. The pope won, took away all Perugia's independence and built a huge castle, the Rocca Paolina, on top of the city quarter where the rich Baglioni family had previously lived. It is said, perhaps apocryphally, that the absence of salt in the region's traditional bread dates from this point.

Artistic and intellectual growth

Given the misery and violence of everyday life in late medieval times, the flourishing of the arts seems incongruous, but it was around this time that the Renaissance court of Federico da Montefeltro became a famous centre of artistic patronage. Pietro Vannucci, better known as Perugino, was born in Città della Pieve in 1446; 37 years later his most famous student, Raphael, was born – the son of an artist at the Urbino court.

It was also a period of wider intellectual flowering. The first copy of Dante's *Divine Comedy* was printed in Foligno, in southern Umbria, in 1472, by which time universities were already thriving in Perugia and Macerata. It may have felt like an era of change and hopefulness, but it wasn't to last.

Under the firm but distant thumb of papal rule the region largely stagnated – isolated, rural and forgotten – until unification.

The Risorgimento to the present day

The Salt War was the final struggle of years of discord between the *comuni* and the papacy. Nearly 200 years earlier Pope Innocent VI had employed Cardinal Albornoz to subdue the region, and many of the papal fortresses he had built still lord it over towns such as Assisi and Spoleto today.

After Perugia finally caved in to the power of the papacy, the region entered a slow decline, though some towns, such as Urbino and Città di Castello, did manage to retain some independence for a while. In many ways this mirrored the fate of Italy in general – after the Renaissance, the European cultural and political status of the whole peninsula began to ebb away to the north.

Between the 16th and 18th centuries Umbria and Marche became something of a backwater. Depopulated and riven by banditry – in the late 16th century the papacy executed over 1000 bandits a year – the area languished as a largely unloved and isolated source of papal taxation. At the end of the 18th century Napoleon came and took control, then left again after a brief period of economic growth, having plundered the region's art and other treasures.

Unification and war

When, in 1859, Perugia rose up in favour of the Risorgimento (the movement to unify Italy), it can have come as no great surprise. When unification finally arrived, the inhabitants of the city celebrated by immediately demolishing the huge Rocca Paolina, the castle that had represented so many years of papal rule.

Despite the revival of the name 'Umbria' in 1870, life under the new Italian Republic was not much easier than before. Opened up to national competition after centuries of torpor, the Umbrian and Marche economies struggled to cope. And when, in the early 20th century, opportunities to escape presented themselves, thousands did so, emigrating to America in huge numbers. Those left behind turned increasingly to socialism and communism in search of economic solutions, though their hopes of change were dashed under the regime of Mussolini, who left his profile built into the Marche rocks at the Gola del Furlo (see page 23). In the Second World War Foligno was badly bombed by Allied forces, as was Terni, whose armaments factories made it a strategic target. Many towns were also left scarred when the German forces retreated, destroying infrastructure as they went.

Reinvention

In the second half of the 20th century, despite continued emigration, civic pride returned as power filtered down to the regions, and Umbria and Marche began to benefit from tourism and small-scale business. Transport links were improved, and cultural events – from revived medieval festivals to new seasons of jazz and opera – brought some zest to the area. Also important has been the renaissance of Umbrian food, which is increasingly exported to the rest of Italy and beyond.

The 1997 Umbrian earthquake, and the 2009 earthquake in neighbouring Abruzzo, were setbacks for a region increasingly reliant on tourism. For some years people stayed away, and there was also some disquiet over the way money was channelled into big projects and not into re-housing the homeless. Now, however, Most Marchigiani look to the future with some optimism: theirs is a region finally on the up.

Art and architecture

Though it is a region often defined by its verdant landscape, what makes Umbria and Marche so special is the way that humans have interacted with this landscape for the last 2500 years, leaving their mark in the forms of buildings, roads and farms. The continuity is remarkable – town walls built before the Roman era have been patched up now and again but still survive, and even where the original structures no longer stand, designs for (and often stones from) buildings erected by the Romans have been reused.

Art, too, has made its mark on the region: Raphael was born here, and some of the most important art ever painted adorns the Basilica of di San Francesco in Assisi. It is a land of religious art, of Perugino, Pinturricchio and the Crivelli brothers, but also of the beginnings of something else: the region's landscape makes some significant appearances, and some of its portraits, such as those of Federico da Montefeltro and his wife Battista Sforza, are instantly recognizable. It's also a region with – somewhat unusually for Italy – some excellent 20th-century art, especially the Burri Collection in Città di Castello and the sculpture and paintings of Spoleto, Marcerata and Ascoli Piceno.

Etruscan and Roman art

Despite the wide spread of the Umbri across the region, they left little of their building and art. The Etruscans, however, seemingly obsessed with death and rituals, left a large body of artefacts in tombs around Umbria, and Romans built upon their legacy.

Richly decorated pottery and carved stone sarcophagi tell us most of what we know of Etruscan civilization. The Museo Archeologico Nazionale in Orvieto has frescoes from two Etruscan tombs, with figures attending a funeral banquet, which show an elegance in Etruscan art that is often overlooked. The tombs themselves, just outside Orvieto, are solid, square, stone structures.

Etruscan pottery
Much of the pottery found in Etruscan tombs comes from Greece. In fact, so keen were the Etruscans on Greek pottery that a lot of it was made with this export market in mind, and more Ancient Greek pottery has been found in Italy than in Greece. In time, the Etruscans copied and developed the Greek styles. Gradually, figures and animals appeared, almost always in profile. Oriental patterns appeared around 700 BC, and the characteristic 'black-figure' pottery, with human figures against a red ground, followed in the same century. This style was subsequently reversed, so that red figures appear against a black background.

Bucchero ware is the black, usually polished, pottery most often associated with the Etruscans, and there are plenty of examples in museums around the region, especially in Orvieto and Perugia. The colour was achieved by firing the pots in an atmosphere of carbon monoxide instead of oxygen. The best pieces are from the seventh and sixth centuries BC, influenced at first by Phoenician and Cypriot designs and later by Greek pottery.

Roman advances
Etruscan towns were designed, rather than growing organically, and had two main axes: the north–south *cardo* and the east-west *decumanus*, dividing each town into four quarters. The form was later adopted by the Romans, who also developed other Etruscan

features, such as barrelled arches, good roads and excellent drainage systems and sewers. Rome had the military might, however, and came to dominate the region, building towns around the important via Flaminia, the road that connected Rome with the Adriatic. The Romans' invention of concrete in the first century BC meant that, while they took up Etruscan forms, their buildings could be bigger and stronger; their use of marble also meant that their decorations and statues were finer, and lasted longer.

Though there are few, if any, intact Roman buildings in the region, there are plenty of ruins, and also many Roman elements that were reused in later buildings. The Tempietto sul Clitunno contains so many Roman elements that it was long considered to be a Roman structure; the entire front section of the Temple of Minerva in Assisi was retained when it became a church; and the Basilica di San Salvatore in Spoleto uses Roman columns, capitals and carvings in a comically haphazard fashion.

Medieval art and architecture

After the Romans, art and architecture suffered for centuries – medieval works were either forgotten, or were destroyed in the many battles, and little of that period survives today. From around AD 1000 to the start of the Renaissance the conflict continued, but despite the Guelph-Ghibelline chaos (see page 71), or in some cases because of it, towns began to grow and prosper.

Competition between rival towns, and between Church and State, led to unprecedented architectural and artistic one-upmanship. While the wealthier and more powerful Church built bigger churches and cathedrals, towns such as Gubbio tried to exert their independence by building bigger and more impressive town halls and public buildings. Increased private wealth amongst merchants also meant that grand homes were constructed.

Byzantine art
The Church employed artists to decorate its new buildings, initially in a largely Byzantine style, with front-on portraits of the Madonna and Child on patterned backgrounds of gold leaf. As the period wore on, these became more sophisticated, culminating in the extraordinary storytelling frescoes of Giotto and Cimabue in the Basilica di San Francesco in Assisi, a crucial stepping-stone in the path towards the Renaissance and a modern concept of art.

From Romanesque to Gothic
This was also a time of changing styles in architecture. The Romanesque style, so-called because it used many of the round forms of ancient Roman architecture, can be seen in some of the region's oldest churches, such as at San Pietro in Valle and Sant'Eufemia in Spoleto both largely constructed in the 12th century. Buildings of this type combine sturdy walls with round arches, barrel vaults and large towers. Their symmetrical layouts are generally simple and their windows small.

Gothic style, which originated in France, was long regarded as inferior in central Italy – indeed the Italians coined the description 'Gothic' as an insult, because they equated the style with something barbaric. Nevertheless, it became increasingly influential, with its more complex ribbed vaulting, flying buttresses, pointed arches and high, light, stained-glass windows. The upper church in the Basilica di San Francesco is a good example of Umbrian Gothic at its best.

As Umbria and Marche came under papal control, political influence and power drained away; many towns in the region stagnated after the 15th century, retaining their medieval buildings and traditions. Wander around the centres of Umbrian hill towns such as Gubbio, Perugia or Assisi, and you might feel that in 500 years nothing much has changed.

The Renaissance

After the often flat, decorative, Byzantineinfluenced religious art of the medieval period, the artistic flowering of the Renaissance in the 15th century was a dramatic change. Influenced by the work of Giotto and a rediscovery of the forms and shapes understood in ancient Roman times, artists started painting three-dimensional space, light and shadow, rendering architectural perspective and including landscape and domestic detail. Though most art remained nominally religious, contemporary faces and emotions appeared in works that were often paid for by rich families. This patronage in turn created a cult of personality, and painters – who had previously been largely anonymous – became the celebrities of the age.

Umbria's great artists

Pietro Vannucci, known as Perugino, was born in Città della Pieve in 1446. His work marks the beginning, and arguably the apotheosis, of the so-called Umbrian school of Renaissance art. Perugino worked in the studio of Andrea del Verrocchio, alongside Leonardo da Vinci, and he may have also studied under Piero della Francesca. His greatest achievement was probably his tutoring of Raphael, though at his peak he also produced some great Renaissance art, before falling back into saccharine cliché later in his career. He was one of the most famous and successful painters of the time, and was called to Rome by the pope to paint the Sistine Chapel.

The Umbrian landscape, notably around the shores of Lake Trasimeno, features strongly in Perugino's art, and he clearly took his studies of perspective seriously. It is easy to see links between his painting and that of his pupil Raphael, but it is also possible to see how Raphael improved on what he had learnt.

Pinturicchio was a contemporary (and assistant) of Perugino, and is often overshadowed by him, sometimes rather unfairly. Though he was not an innovator like Perugino, Pinturicchio's decorative paintings exhibit a detached, careful draughtsmanship that has aged well and often appears quite contemporary next to Perugino's sentimentality. Born Bernardino di Betto in Perugia in 1454, Pinturicchio worked with Perugino on frescoes in the Sistine Chapel and later decorated rooms in the Vatican Library. His finely observed plants and landscapes mark him out as an artist with a very keen eye, and many of his paintings are embellished with fascinating minutiae.

Raffaello Sanzio (known in English as Raphael) was born in Urbino in 1483. His father Giovanni Santi was also an accomplished painter and poet, and was court artist to Federico da Montefeltro. Raphael was orphaned at the age of 11, but by then he had already worked with his father, and as a teenager he showed precocious talent. There is debate about when he worked as an assistant, and perhaps as an apprentice, to Perugino in Perugia, but by 1501 he was already described as a fully trained master. The depiction of Daniel in one of Perugino's sumptuous paintings in the Collegio del Cambio is probably a portrait of Raphael, and his own first documented fresco is also in Perugia, in the Cappella di San Severo.

Renaissance architecture

Though the region's great architecture is mainly medieval, there are some notable Renaissance buildings too, such as La Fortezza in San Leo (see page 24) and the Palazzo

Ducale in Urbino (see page 19). Many medieval buildings, such as the Cattedrale di Santa Maria Assunta in Spoleto were given Renaissance additions.

Post-Renaissance

Under papal rule, the region's art and architecture largely stagnated for centuries. This lack of development has left many artistic treasures unspoilt, but it has also stunted artistic life. A 20th-century rebirth of sorts centred around Alberto Burri in Città di Castello. His abstract sculptures, full of pain and suffering, were a response to the violence of the period. His legacy has left sculpture as one of the region's foremost artistic outlets – Arnaldo Pomodoro's sculpture park and museum at Castello di Pietrarubbia in Marche (see page 25) is a fine example.

Burri's use of post-industrial space in the tobacco-drying sheds of Città di Castello is also one of the region's best examples of contemporary architecture. A drive through the ugly suburbs of Perugia or Ancona provides graphic evidence that interesting architecture of modern times is concentrated on reusing existing structures rather than on building beautiful new ones.

Contents

Footnotes

Language

In hotels and bigger restaurants, you'll usually find English is spoken. The further you go from the tourist centres, however, the more trouble you may have, unless you have at least a smattering of Italian.

Italians from the rest of the country often consider modern-day Marchigiani to speak with a rather slow, rural Italian, and though such attitudes are exaggerated, you may be able to detect a country lilt to some spoken language in the region. That said, it's seldom hard to understand.

Marchigiano dialect still exists, especially in rural areas, and sometimes in the names of traditional local dishes.

Vowels

a	like 'a' in cat	i	like 'i' in sip (except after c or g, see below)
e	like 'e' in vet, or slightly more open, like the 'ai' in air (except after c or g, see consonants below)	o	like 'o' in fox
		u	like 'ou' in soup

Consonants

Generally consonants sound the same as in English, though 'e' and 'i' after 'c' or 'g' make them soft (a 'ch' or a 'j' sound) and are silent themselves, whereas 'h' makes them hard (a 'k' or 'g' sound), the opposite to English. So ciao is pronounced 'chaow', but chiesa (church) is pronounced 'kee-ay-sa'.

The combination 'gli' is pronounced like the 'lli' in million, and 'gn' like 'ny' in Tanya.

Basics

thank you	*grazie*	goodnight	*buonanotte*
hi/goodbye	*ciao* (informal)	goodbye	*arrivederci*
good day		please	*per favore*
(until after lunch/		I'm sorry	*mi dispiace*
mid-afternoon)	*buongiorno*	excuse me	*permesso*
good evening		yes	*sì*
(after lunch)	*buonasera*	no	*no*

Numbers

1	*uno*	17	*diciassette*
2	*due*	18	*diciotto*
3	*tre*	19	*diciannove*
4	*quattro*	20	*venti*
5	*cinque*	21	*ventuno*
6	*sei*	22	*ventidue*
7	*sette*	30	*trenta*
8	*otto*	40	*quaranta*
9	*nove*	50	*cinquanta*
10	*dieci*	60	*sessanta*
11	*undici*	70	*settanta*
12	*dodici*	80	*ottanta*
13	*tredici*	90	*novanta*
14	*quattordici*	100	*cento*
15	*quindici*	200	*due cento*
16	*sedici*	1000	*mille*

Gestures

Italians are famously theatrical and animated in dialogue and use a variety of gestures.

Side of left palm on side of right wrist as right wrist is flicked up Go away

Hunched shoulders and arms lifted with palms of hands outwards What am I supposed to do?

Thumb, index and middle finger of hand together, wrist upturned and shaking What are you doing/what's going on?

Both palms together and moved up and down in front of stomach Same as above

All fingers of hand squeezed together To signify a place is packed full of people

Front or side of hand to chin 'Nothing', as in 'I don't understand' or 'I've had enough'

Flicking back of right ear To signify someone is gay

Index finger in cheek To signify good food

Questions

how?	*come?*	where?	*dove?*
how much?	*quanto?*	why?	*perché?*
when?	*quando?*	what?	*che cosa?*

Problems

I don't understand	*non capisco*
I don't know	*non lo so*
I don't speak Italian	*non parlo italiano*
How do you say ... (in Italian)?	*come si dice ... (in italiano)?*
Is there anyone who speaks English?	*c'è qualcuno che parla inglese?*

Shopping

this one/that one	*questo/quello*
less	*meno*
more	*di più*
how much is it/are they?	*quanto costa/costano?*
can I have ...?	*posso avere ...?*

Travelling

one ticket for...	*un biglietto per...*
single	*solo andata*
return	*andata e ritorno*
does this go to Como?	*questo va a Como?*
airport	*aeroporto*
bus stop	*fermata*
train	*treno*
car	*macchina*
taxi	*tassi*

Hotels

a double/single room	*una camera doppia/singola*
a double bed	*un letto matrimoniale*
bathroom	*bagno*
Is there a view?	*c'è un bel panorama?*
can I see the room?	*posso vedere la camera?*
when is breakfast?	*a che ora è la colazione?*
can I have the key?	*posso avere la chiave?*

Restaurants

can I have the bill please?	*posso avere il conto per favore?*
is there a menu?	*c'è un menù?*
what do you recommend?	*che cosa mi consegna?*
what's this?	*cos'è questo?*
where's the toilet?	*dov'è il bagno?*

Time

morning	*mattina*
afternoon	*pomeriggio*
evening	*sera*
night	*notte*
soon	*presto/fra poco*
later	*più tardi*
what time is it?	*che ore sono?*
today/tomorrow/yesterday	*oggi/domani/ieri*

Days

Monday	*lunedi*
Tuesday	*martedi*
Wednesday	*mercoledi*
Thursday	*giovedi*
Friday	*venerdi*
Saturday	*sabato*
Sunday	*domenica*

Conversation

alright	*va bene*
right then	*allora*
who knows!	*bo!/chi sa*
good luck!	*in bocca al lupo!*
	(literally, 'in the mouth of the wolf')
one moment	*un attimo*
hello (when answering a phone)	*pronto* (literally, 'ready')
let's go!	*andiamo!*
enough/stop	*basta!*
give up!	*dai!*
I like ...	*mi piace ...*
how's it going?	*come va?*
(well, thanks)	(*bene, grazie*)
how are you?	*come sta/stai?* (polite/informal)

Menu reader

General

affumicato smoked
al sangue rare
alla griglia grilled
antipasto starter/appetizer
aperto/chiuso open/closed
arrosto roasted
ben cotto well done
bollito boiled
caldo hot
cameriere/cameriera waiter/waitress
conto the bill
contorni side dishes
coperto cover charge
coppa/cono cone/cup
cotto cooked
cottura media medium
crudo raw
degustazione tasting menu of several dishes
dolce dessert
fatto in casa home-made
forno a legna wood-fired oven
freddo cold
fresco fresh, uncooked
fritto fried
menu turistico tourist menu
piccante spicy
prenotazione reservation
primo first course
ripieno a stuffing or something that is stuffed
secondo second course

Drinks (*bevande*)

acqua naturale/gassata/frizzante
  still/sparkling water
aperitivo drinks taken before dinner,
  often served with free snacks
bicchiere glass
birra beer
birra alla spina draught beer
bottiglia bottle
caffè coffee (ie espresso)
caffè macchiato/ristretto espresso with a
  dash of foamed milk/strong
spremuta freshly squeezed fruit juice
succo juice
vino bianco/rosato/rosso white/rosé/red wine

Fruit (*frutta*) and vegetables (*legumi*)

agrumi citrus fruits
amarena sour cherry
arancia orange
carciofio globe artichoke
castagne chestnuts
cipolle onions
cocomero water melon
contorno side dish, usually grilled
  vegetables or oven-baked potatoes
fichi figs
finocchio fennel
fragole strawberries
friarelli strong flavoured leaves of the
  broccoli family eaten with sausages
frutta fresca fresh fruit
funghi mushroom
lamponi raspberries
melagrana pomegranate
melanzana eggplant/aubergine
melone light coloured melon
mele apples
noci/nocciole walnuts/hazelnuts
patate potatoes, which can be *arroste* (roast),
  fritte (fried), *novelle* (new), *pure' di* (mashed)
patatine fritte chips
peperoncino chilli pepper
peperone peppers
pesche peaches
piselli peas
pomodoro tomato
rucola rocket
scarola leafy green vegetable used in
  torta di scarola pie
sciurilli or *fiorilli* tempura courgette flowers
spinaci spinach
verdure vegetables
zucca pumpkin

Meat (*carne*)

affettati misti mixed cured meat
agnello lamb
bistecca beef steak

bresaola thinly sliced, air-cured beef from Valtellina

carpaccio finely sliced raw meat (usually beef)

cinghiale boar

coda alla vaccinara oxtail

coniglio rabbit

involtini thinly sliced meat, rolled and stuffed

manzo beef

pollo chicken

polpette meatballs

polpettone meat loaf

porchetta roasted whole suckling pig

prosciutto ham – *cotto* cooked, *crudo* cured

salsicce pork sausage

salumi cured meats, usually served mixed (*salumi misto*) on a wooden platter

speck a type of cured, smoked ham

spiedini meat pieces grilled on a skewer

stufato meat stew

trippa tripe

vitello veal

Fish (*pesce*) and seafood (*frutti di mare*)

acciughe anchovies

aragosta lobster

baccalà salt cod

bottarga mullet-roe

branzino sea bass

calamari squid

cozze mussels

frittura di mare/frittura di paranza small fish, squid and shellfish lightly covered with flour and fried

frutti di mare seafood

gamberi shrimps/prawns

grigliata mista di pesce mixed grilled fish

orata gilt-head/sea bream

ostriche oysters

pesce spada swordfish

polpo octopus

sarde, sardine sardines

seppia cuttlefish

sogliola sole

spigola bass

stoccafisso stockfish

tonno tuna

triglia red mullet

trota trout

vongole clams

Dessert (*dolce*)

cornetto sweet croissant

crema custard

dolce dessert

gelato ice cream

granita flavoured crushed ice

macedonia (di frutta) fruit cocktail dessert with white wine

panettone type of fruit bread eaten at Christmas

semifreddo a partially frozen dessert

sorbetto sorbet

tiramisù rich 'pick-me-up' dessert

torta cake

zabaglione whipped egg yolks flavoured with Marsala wine

zuppa inglese English-style trifle

Other

aceto balsamico balsamic vinegar, usually from Modena

arborio type of rice used to make risotto

burro butter

calzone pizza dough rolled with the chef's choice of filling and then baked

casatiello lard bread

fagioli white beans

formaggi misti mixed cheese plate

formaggio cheese

frittata omelette

insalata salad

insalata Caprese salad of tomatoes, mozzarella and basil

latte milk

lenticchie lentils

mandorla almond

miele honey

olio oil

polenta cornmeal

pane bread

pane-integrale brown bread

pinoli pine nuts

provola cheese, sometimes with a smoky flavour

ragù a meaty sauce or ragout

riso rice

salsa sauce

sugo sauce or gravy

zuppa soup

Index

Titles available in the Footprint *Focus* range

Latin America	UK RRP	US RRP
Bahia & Salvador	£7.99	$11.95
Brazilian Amazon	£7.99	$11.95
Brazilian Pantanal	£6.99	$9.95
Buenos Aires & Pampas	£7.99	$11.95
Cartagena & Caribbean Coast	£7.99	$11.95
Costa Rica	£8.99	$12.95
Cuzco, La Paz & Lake Titicaca	£8.99	$12.95
El Salvador	£5.99	$8.95
Guadalajara & Pacific Coast	£6.99	$9.95
Guatemala	£8.99	$12.95
Guyana, Guyane & Suriname	£5.99	$8.95
Havana	£6.99	$9.95
Honduras	£7.99	$11.95
Nicaragua	£7.99	$11.95
Northeast Argentina & Uruguay	£8.99	$12.95
Paraguay	£5.99	$8.95
Quito & Galápagos Islands	£7.99	$11.95
Recife & Northeast Brazil	£7.99	$11.95
Rio de Janeiro	£8.99	$12.95
São Paulo	£5.99	$8.95
Uruguay	£6.99	$9.95
Venezuela	£8.99	$12.95
Yucatán Peninsula	£6.99	$9.95

Asia	UK RRP	US RRP
Angkor Wat	£5.99	$8.95
Bali & Lombok	£8.99	$12.95
Chennai & Tamil Nadu	£8.99	$12.95
Chiang Mai & Northern Thailand	£7.99	$11.95
Goa	£6.99	$9.95
Gulf of Thailand	£8.99	$12.95
Hanoi & Northern Vietnam	£8.99	$12.95
Ho Chi Minh City & Mekong Delta	£7.99	$11.95
Java	£7.99	$11.95
Kerala	£7.99	$11.95
Kolkata & West Bengal	£5.99	$8.95
Mumbai & Gujarat	£8.99	$12.95

Africa & Middle East	UK RRP	US RRP
Beirut	£6.99	$9.95
Cairo & Nile Delta	£8.99	$12.95
Damascus	£5.99	$8.95
Durban & KwaZulu Natal	£8.99	$12.95
Fès & Northern Morocco	£8.99	$12.95
Jerusalem	£8.99	$12.95
Johannesburg & Kruger National Park	£7.99	$11.95
Kenya's Beaches	£8.99	$12.95
Kilimanjaro & Northern Tanzania	£8.99	$12.95
Luxor to Aswan	£8.99	$12.95
Nairobi & Rift Valley	£7.99	$11.95
Red Sea & Sinai	£7.99	$11.95
Zanzibar & Pemba	£7.99	$11.95

Europe	UK RRP	US RRP
Bilbao & Basque Region	£6.99	$9.95
Brittany West Coast	£7.99	$11.95
Cádiz & Costa de la Luz	£6.99	$9.95
Granada & Sierra Nevada	£6.99	$9.95
Languedoc: Carcassonne to Montpellier	£7.99	$11.95
Málaga	£5.99	$8.95
Marseille & Western Provence	£7.99	$11.95
Orkney & Shetland Islands	£5.99	$8.95
Santander & Picos de Europa	£7.99	$11.95
Sardinia: Alghero & the North	£7.99	$11.95
Sardinia: Cagliari & the South	£7.99	$11.95
Seville	£5.99	$8.95
Sicily: Palermo & the Northwest	£7.99	$11.95
Sicily: Catania & the Southeast	£7.99	$11.95
Siena & Southern Tuscany	£7.99	$11.95
Sorrento, Capri & Amalfi Coast	£6.99	$9.95
Skye & Outer Hebrides	£6.99	$9.95
Verona & Lake Garda	£7.99	$11.95

North America	UK RRP	US RRP
Vancouver & Rockies	£8.99	$12.95

Australasia	UK RRP	US RRP
Brisbane & Queensland	£8.99	$12.95
Perth	£7.99	$11.95

For the latest books, e-books and a wealth of travel information, visit us at: www.footprinttravelguides.com.

Join us on facebook for the latest travel news, product releases, offers and amazing competitions: www.facebook.com/footprintbooks.